Fashion
Designers
at the **Opera**

Fashion Designers
at the Opera

HELENA MATHEOPOULOS

With 202 illustrations, 195 in colour

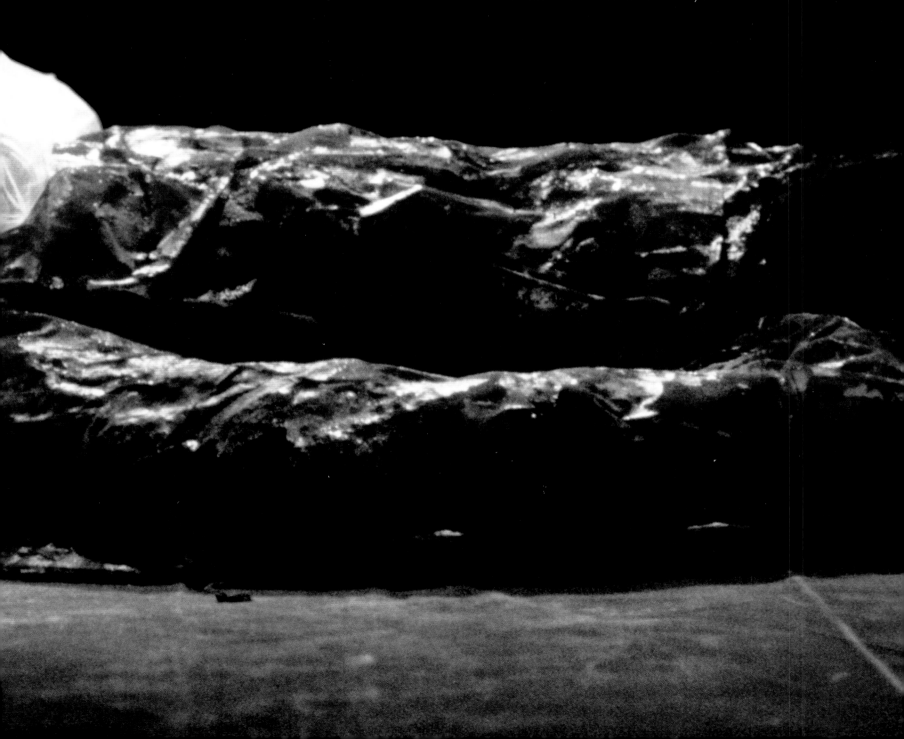

To the memory of Dominique de Borchgrave,
unique, unforgettable – and equally clothesaholic – friend

CONTENTS

INTRODUCTION

'It's called creative tension and it's what happens when the worlds of opera and fashion collide!'

These words were published in the UK *Sunday Times* newspaper in 1995, a few days before the premiere of *Così fan tutte* that marked Sir Jonathan Miller's eagerly awaited Covent Garden debut, featuring costumes designed by Giorgio Armani.

This electrifying and rewarding collision has occurred more and more frequently in recent years, with fashion designers *en masse* falling in love with opera. 'Opera makes your spirit and mind soar.... Maybe this is what I should do if I wasn't already in my dream job!' enthused John Galliano, who produced some stunning costumes for the celebrated American soprano Renée Fleming to wear at a Metropolitan Opera gala in 2008. Gianni Versace concurred, noting, 'You can sing with designs on stage.' He was evidently right, because in 2009 and 2010 alone Tom Ford, Christian Lacroix, Miuccia Prada, Emanuel Ungaro and Viktor & Rolf made successful sorties as costumiers for high-profile operatic productions across the globe.

'It's been my experience that fashion designers love designing for the stage and for opera,' commented Renée Fleming, 'because we are highly theatrical.... I have to remind people that the word "diva" originated with us in the nineteenth century. It just means "goddess"...and who wouldn't want to dress a goddess?'

However, unlike the long tradition linking fashion with the ballet, dating back to the 1920s and Diaghilev's Ballets Russes, the love affair between fashion and opera is a comparatively recent phenomenon. There was the odd exception in the early twentieth century, with Lucile, for example, designing spectacular costumes in London for *The Merry Widow*. But it was not until 1980 that the collaboration began in earnest, with Karl Lagerfeld producing the costumes for *Les Contes d'Hoffmann* at the Maggio Musicale Fiorentino, and Giorgio Armani for *Erwartung* at La Scala. Two years later, Lagerfeld designed *Les Troyens*, also at La Scala. In 1983 Ottavio and Rosita Missoni created the costumes for a very 'Scottish' production of *Lucia di Lammermoor* at La Scala and the Grand Théâtre de Genève. The following year, again for La Scala, Gianni Versace produced designs for *Don Pasquale*. Around the same time, Marc Bohan, then Creative Director of Dior, was designing *Orfeo ed Euridice* in Monte Carlo. Within a few years, Christian Lacroix, one of the most theatrical and operatically erudite of designers, had followed suit with *Carmen* at the Arènes de Nîmes.

By the turn of the millennium, Zandra Rhodes had begun her expansion into the field with costumes for *The Magic Flute* at San Diego. By the end of the 2010 season, Emanuel Ungaro had designed the costumes for two productions – *La Damnation de Faust* and *La clemenza di Tito* – at the Teatro San Carlo in Naples; Viktor & Rolf had been chosen by the director Robert Wilson for his magical staging of *Der Freischütz* at Baden-Baden; Tom Ford, formerly Creative Director of Gucci and now a distinguished film director, had designed the costumes for the world premiere of *The Letter*, based on a novella by Somerset Maugham, at the Santa Fe Opera Festival; and Miuccia Prada had

OPPOSITE Renée Fleming in the title role of the Metropolitan Opera production of Jules Massenet's *Thaïs*, New York, 2009, with costumes designed by Christian Lacroix.

made her first foray into opera with a production of *Attila* in no less a venue than the Metropolitan Opera in New York. In 2010, meanwhile, Christian Lacroix, who had been a constant presence on the operatic stage for well over a decade, designed a highly acclaimed production of *Agrippina* for the Berlin State Opera, with *Candide* in the pipeline for Berlin, *Aida* for Cologne and *Carmen* for Stockholm. Emanuel Ungaro, meantime, has been preparing *La traviata* for the historic, newly restored Teatro Petruzzelli in Bari.

Opera is undoubtedly the new favourite, among fashion designers both of haute couture and ready to wear. Their involvement with this most 'theatrical' of arts seems to be gaining momentum every year, parallel to their extensive involvement in the pop music industry. But, diva worship apart, what lies behind this new trend? Why, in a fashion world dominated and influenced by 'rock chick chic', are so many designers tempted to the operatic stage, some on a regular and others on a one-off basis? What is the appeal of this magical art form for designers as disparate as Giorgio Armani, who thinks that 'less is more', and the late Gianni Versace, who thought that 'less is a snore'?

The principal reason is the revolution that has radically transformed both fashion and opera and narrowed the borderline between the two worlds. The past quarter-century has seen the steady transformation of fashion into 'costume' in terms of inspiration, and 'shows' in terms of display. Unlike the couture presentations of yesteryear, which aimed to sell real-life clothes to real women, today's fashion shows resemble themed theatrical spectacles and brim with extravagant, 'fantasy' clothes, often indistinguishable from costumes and sometimes not meant to be worn, or even manufactured.

The past forty or so years, meanwhile, have seen the total transformation of opera as an art form. The 'Callas Revolution' turned opera into believable theatre and enabled it to survive and even thrive in an era dominated by cinematic criteria of dramatic credibility by making it attractive to younger audiences. Until the advent of Maria Callas (and directors such as Luchino Visconti and Wieland Wagner), opera was vocally resplendent but usually dramatically ridiculous. The Callas Revolution changed beyond recognition the very nature of operatic interpretation and, through Callas's own transformation into a sylph, the physical appearance of opera singers. Gone are the 'fat ladies' of old, whose looks precluded any serious scenic acting or identification with their roles. In the last thirty years they have been replaced by a new generation of divas – Renée Fleming, Angela Gheorghiu, Susan Graham, Joyce DiDonato, Nina Stemme, Anna Netrebko, Natalie Dessay and Danielle de Niese, to name but a few – who look as beautiful as they sound. They could easily double as film stars, and are thus able to tempt fashion designers to the operatic stage. As John Galliano said of Fleming: 'She is such an inspiring, vibrant, exciting performer! I love the energy and cool she is bringing to opera. Her voice with its whole palette of colours, emotions and tones…made me want to create something bold, vivacious, sensual and capricious.'

It goes without saying, of course, that each designer also has personal reasons for their involvement in opera. Some, such as Christian Lacroix, Emanuel Ungaro and Marc Bohan, were opera lovers from a young age. Others, including Zandra Rhodes, came to it much later and initially accepted the challenge because they appreciated the 'wider canvas' that opera offered compared to fashion. Working in opera allows the designers' creative imaginations a respite from commercial restrictions and enables them to operate on a purely artistic level. This may be why, for example, Lacroix, Lagerfeld and Galliano each agreed to design one act of an opera for Renée Fleming's Metropolitan Opera Gala without being paid a fee, but instead working at cost.

However, along with the fun – and, of course, the prestige – of being invited to participate in an operatic production, the designers are also confronted by a basic question: how does designing for the stage differ from designing a fashion collection, both technically and conceptually?

One of the first technical lessons that has to be learned is how to ensure that the costumes make an impact from afar, instead of up close, with the focus on detail that is so vital in fashion. This 'broad brush' treatment usually involves the designers using fabrics they would never dream of working with when creating couture or ready-to-wear garments. They must also design in a way that allows singers to move freely and keep cool, since the act of singing produces terrific body heat.

On a conceptual level, one might think that the designers would experience some frustration in their new role. Instead of being the boss – the emperor of a domain over which they are used to reigning supreme – they are now reduced to a supporting role that compels them to subjugate their own will and vision to that of the stage director, whose concept they must interpret in visual terms. Surprisingly, this loss of control seems to hold great appeal for some. As Lacroix comments: 'In fashion, I used to be the only "captain on board", with my personal, even selfish approach. But in opera, I never try to act as if I, myself, were the director. I have to accept his view instead of imposing my own. It is he who decides what the concept will be, and I am there to provide illustrations to his imagination. But subordinating my will to the director's is one of the things I find most rewarding about working in the theatre. I have to be more humble and less egotistical than I used to be as a couturier.'

Perhaps this is why famous operatic directors tend to speak positively about fashion designers as costumiers. Vincent Boussard said of his longstanding collaboration with Lacroix, 'He is always after something new, something different. He transforms my concept and makes it stronger.' Robert Wilson's verdict on his experience of working with Viktor & Rolf was that 'they brought their own world to my world. The choice of materials was their own invention and a great complement to my scenic elements.' Wilson's memory of the late, much-lamented Gianni Versace is that he was 'a perfectionist, who paid meticulous attention to detail and whose artistic integrity was matched by his openmindedness. With him, you truly felt part of a team. I would have loved to have worked with him again. I think he would have been brilliant for *Aida*, and also a sensational designer for *Lulu*.' Pierre Audi was similarly impressed by his collaboration with Miuccia Prada on the Metropolitan Opera's *Attila*: 'Her work is musical and innovative in its simplicity and power. It combines the right degree of poetry and meaning, which opera needs to thrive on if it is to survive the twenty-first century.'

Singers also tend to be enthusiastic about having their costumes created by fashion designers. As Renée Fleming noted: 'I sewed my prom dress, so I can really appreciate what they are doing. When you see the degree of imagination and talent that these [designers] have brought to these costumes, it becomes obvious why they are who they are. It's a different level. The thing that stands out is the imagination – there is a fantasy that is quite extraordinary....'

The verdict of opera-house managements has been equally positive. Each time a collaboration with a major designer is announced, an enormous 'buzz' is created, not only among opera lovers, but also among a wider audience who may never before have set foot in an opera house, and also among the media, and this in turn attracts celebrities. Everybody benefits. The only question now is: who's next?

Giorgio Armani

'Stark, contemporary sets were ideally suited to my aesthetic concepts'

According to Nicholas Payne, Opera Director of the Royal Opera House at the time of Covent Garden's famous collaborations with two of the world's top fashion designers, 'Very few opera directors have ever been brave or humble enough to link their ego with that of an equally famous name to theirs. John Cox did it for his production of Richard Strauss's *Capriccio* [he invited Gianni Versace to design the costumes], and Jonathan Miller did it when he persuaded Giorgio Armani to provide the clothes for his 1995 production of Mozart's *Così fan tutte*.'

In both cases, the designers in question were not just well-known; they were worldwide household names. The moment each collaboration was announced, the news caused, to quote a local newspaper, 'as much interest as the birth of a new diva'. Audiences flocked to Covent Garden, and subsequent press coverage eclipsed the usual reviews in the arts pages of national newspapers. The premiere, which was attended by a starry audience, and the party that was hosted by Armani after a later performance, filled the gossip columns of the tabloid press and glossy magazines for weeks.

Armani's only previous foray onto the operatic stage had been to provide a stunning dress for the heroine of Schoenberg's one-act monodrama, *Erwartung*, produced at La Scala in 1980–81 (see pp. 2–3). His collaboration with the Royal Opera came about as the result of a brainwave on the part of Jonathan Miller, who, after directing scores of acclaimed productions at the English National Opera and worldwide, was finally making his debut at Covent Garden. Miller would almost certainly never have agreed to direct a revival of an old production of *Così fan tutte*, but the Royal Opera had virtually no budget for a new production. When, over a lunch with Miller, Payne mentioned the figure available – barely £30,000 for both sets *and* costumes – he half-expected no for an answer. But, to his surprise and relief, after a pause for reflection, Miller accepted, 'provided he was allowed to design and practically build the sets himself in our technical department' – which he eventually did, with the aid of five assistants.

Miller had directed several 'classic' productions of Mozart operas, set in their proper period (including his landmark staging of *Le nozze di Figaro* at the 1990 Vienna Festival), but for *Così fan tutte* he wanted a modern staging that would bring home the relevance of this sparkling 'comedy' for every age. '*Così* is a timeless story,' he says. 'It doesn't happen anywhere in particular; it happens everywhere. And that's what I wanted to put across in this production.' On the subject of the opera's themes, he adds, 'In my view, the piece is not about fidelity. It's about identity, about disguise or, if you like, the danger of disguise. At the back of my mind was a story my mother wrote at the end of the war about how differently people behaved the moment they were in uniform. Disguised people become someone else and do things they wouldn't normally do.... In the process, they may even discover they *are* someone else, someone different from the person they thought they were.'

OPPOSITE Sketch of a dress from the 1997 Emporio Armani collection, used in the revival of Jonathan Miller's production of Mozart's *Così fan tutte* at Covent Garden. When the production first opened, in 1995, Miller and the Royal Opera House team chose Armani designs because they wanted to feature 'clothes' rather than 'costumes' in their modern-day production.

While *Le nozze di Figaro* was based on the most scandalous play of its day, Beaumarchais's *La folle journée, ou Le mariage de Figaro*, *Così fan tutte* was an original invented story. As Nicholas Payne notes, 'In this particular case, a modern production seems almost truer to its spirit than setting it in period sets and costumes.' Having decided on this point of view, and bearing in mind the non-existent budget, the team thought, why not have the cast wear real clothes rather than specially designed costumes? Miller suggested asking a well-known fashion house, such as Armani (he passed the Emporio Armani boutique on his way to the opera house), if they would be interested in supplying the clothes. After all, a Covent Garden production would be good promotion for them, so they might consider giving the clothes to the Royal Opera for free.

So Armani was approached, and, as Payne recalls, quite a complicated negotiation ensued because, of course, a successful fashion house has a bevy of publicity, management and marketing people, all intent on protecting 'The Master' and all trying to drive a hard bargain. Naturally, what they wanted was for Armani to design a special range of costumes for the production. Eventually, Payne felt he had to come completely clean with them. 'I said, "Look, if we were to commission a whole set of costumes from you it would cost a lot of money, which we don't have. We've come to you *because* we have no money. On the other hand, Armani's 1995 ready-to-wear collection will receive a huge promotion by appearing on the Covent Garden stage, which you can capitalize on in any way you wish." So eventually the publicity, management and marketing people took the proposal to Armani himself and he said yes, he would do it.'

Armani accepted because he felt that Miller's concept of a modern *Così* in a contemporary setting was in tune with his own design philosophy and style. 'Jonathan Miller and Covent Garden wanted my clothes because they consider them a symbol of contemporary fashion. I don't "do" opera, because operatic productions tend to be in period costumes far removed from modern clothes. I wouldn't be capable of designing an operatic equivalent of *Les liaisons dangereuses*, for instance. But Jonathan Miller wanted to do something modern, elegant, with lots of atmosphere and poetry. I felt inspired by him. It was a pleasure to work with a great director – and one who was so well dressed! The stark, contemporary sets of his production were ideally suited to my aesthetic concepts.'

The main set evoked a photographer's studio – a place that Miller finds inspirational because of its 'white, space-like infinity'. This happened to recall Armani's own pristine, white, seventeenth-century palazzo in Milan, housing his business and design headquarters, his apartment on the top floor, and a tailor-made swimming pool in the basement. It was to this palazzo that Miller strolled for his first meeting with the designer. When Miller arrived, he unthinkingly threw his raincoat down on the sofa. Armani's staff, aware that their obsessively tidy master could not tolerate even a stray hair out of place (he allegedly dictates the number of centimetres between the clothes hangers in his shops), froze and assumed that the collaboration was doomed before it had started. But, as luck would have it, one of Armani's adored Siamese cats saw fit to leap onto the raincoat and, having approved it as a perfect resting place, settled down to a loud purr. As soon as Armani entered the room, he pronounced himself enchanted by the pretty sight, to general sighs of relief....

In the event, the two masters of their arts worked very well together. 'I believe in Jonathan Miller's genius,' declared Armani at the time, while Miller

confirmed that his choice of this least 'theatrical' of designers was well-founded. 'His understated style is the complete opposite of traditional "grand opera" style. This production of *Così fan tutte* violated all the traditions of the Opera House.' According to Nicholas Payne, the point of using Armani outfits was that they were 'just clothes', unlike the garments of a designer such as Lacroix, who loves opera, designs a production almost every season and creates fashion collections which themselves 'are a bit like costumes'. 'In this case,' Payne pointed out, 'we didn't want costumes; we wanted clothes.'

The result of the collaboration was a happy blend of modern tailoring with a few additional theatrical flourishes. The costumes of the two exceptionally good-looking female protagonists – soprano Amanda Roocroft and mezzo Susan Graham (they sang the Neapolitan sisters engaged to two army officers who pretend to go off to war, only to return, disguised, in order to seduce each other's fiancées for the sake of a bet with their worldweary friend, Don Alfonso) – included shell-pink and ice-blue crêpe trouser suits and bustiers, and airy voile skirts, while their maid (or, in this case, studio assistant) Despina wore a crisp tailored trouser suit. The men wore Emporio Armani, with one amusing touch: when they were supposed to go to war, their outfits were topped by UN blue berets, 'as if they were just off to Bosnia', according to Miller. Their later 'Albanian' disguise came out of the Armani collection's 'ethnic look'. To add an even more topical touch, CNN television cameras were on hand to record the men's departure to war, and at one point Don Alfonso, performed with aplomb by Thomas Allen, produced a mobile phone from the pocket of his stylish Armani blazer.

All the clothes were chosen in one afternoon by Jonathan Miller and Covent Garden's appointed costume co-ordinator, Jackie Galloway. She recalls that once the decision to use Emporio Armani had been made and accepted by all concerned, the whole process was concluded very quickly. The clothes were chosen from the spring/summer 1995 collection and submitted to Armani for approval. The only exceptions were the sisters' wedding dresses for the finale, which came from the main Armani couture collection but had special veils added, sprinkled with silver raindrops.

Miller felt that using up-to-date clothing would 'liberate the singers and enable them to go for it'. Interestingly, however, as far as Amanda Roocroft was concerned, this did not happen. She was in fact unable to feel free for a while because, like most performers, she felt the need for 'proper' costumes in order to inhabit her role. 'It was hard to imagine performing in these clothes because I could so easily imagine myself wearing them in real life. Being on stage in the clothes made it feel more like a rehearsal than a real performance. But I just *adored* my baby-blue crêpe trouser suit in Act I. It's just what I would dream of wearing in real life. My eye would go straight to it if I saw it in a shop!'

The production in general, and clothes in particular, provoked similarly effusive reactions in almost everyone. 'The audience said, "Oh, we can go out and buy these clothes", and the cast asked, "Oh, can we keep these clothes?"' Payne particularly remembers Tom Allen being 'very keen on his cashmere jacket'. So desirable were the clothes that backstage security had never been so tight at Covent Garden! Jackie Galloway noted, 'If these were just normal operatic costumes straight out of our own workshop, few would bother to steal them, but anyone who sees the Armani label and thinks they could get

ABOVE Sketch of an Armani couture dress for the Wedding Scene at the finale of the original showing of *Così fan tutte* at Covent Garden in 1995.

OPPOSITE Sketch of a trouser suit from the 1997 Emporio Armani collection, worn by Fiordiligi (sung by Soile Isokoski) in the 1997 revival of *Così fan tutte* at Covent Garden.

away with it would be off with these scrumptious clothes in an instant!' Once the management realized that the clothes' very topicality meant they could not be used for further revivals, the singers were in fact allowed to keep them.

Usually, when a revival is planned, an opera house's wardrobe department brings the costumes out of storage and adjusts them to the measurements of the new cast. In this case, however, Armani's wish was for Covent Garden to use his latest collections every time a new production was staged. He duly supplied new outfits for the first revival in 1997, but he then realized that he could not realistically carry on doing this indefinitely. For the second revival, Miller decided to use clothing from the British high-street store Marks & Spencer.

At the time of the original premiere, Miller had found himself irritated by the excessive publicity surrounding the Armani costumes; he has even said that he prefers the 'nameless' garments of subsequent revivals. However, his fear that the costumes would draw more attention than the dramatic production proved groundless. The costumes overshadowed neither story nor music. They were, in the words of the *Musical Times*, 'only a minor metaphor'. Nicholas Payne confirms that the clothes were not meant to be emblematic of the on-stage personalities. 'They were not trying to say that this character is more this way than the other. The line was that here were two quite fashion-conscious

> ❝ The audience said, "Oh, we can go out and buy these clothes", and the cast asked, "Oh, can we keep these clothes?"

OVERLEAF The modern-day setting for *Così fan tutte* – a photographer's studio – built largely by Jonathan Miller and five assistants in the Royal Opera House technical department. The combined budget for sets and costumes was just £30,000.

sisters having a very nice time somewhere in the Bay of Naples. The clothes, which were casual but stylish modern Italian, were not chosen to indicate that one was more flighty than the other, any more than the boys' clothes were. There are a number of ways of doing *Così*. What we were keen to do was to make it *plausible*. I've always thought that if one tries to take a moralistic view of this opera, and condemns each character for behaving badly, one misses the point. The point is that these are four young people, and the fact is that young people do tend to fall in and out of love very quickly, and do also tend to fall for their friends' friends, and people should not get hot and bothered about this.… At the end of it, they are all a little bit older and a little bit more experienced and a little bit sorrier. This is not a tragedy, but they have all grown up a bit. And that's a very pertinent story, in every day and age.'

The production was extraordinarily successful, and remains the landmark staging of *Così* of recent times. Armani attended the third or fourth performance, after which he gave a magnificent sit-down dinner in the Crush Room of the opera house. It was not, as Payne recalls, 'just the usual four-course meal, but an outstanding menu with exceptional vintage wines, which must have cost more than the entire production. I didn't dare ask, but I bet it did!'

Marc
Bohan

'Designing for the stage is fun because there are rehearsals, and I *love* rehearsals'

Marc Bohan, the distinguished fashion designer who headed the house of Christian Dior and its vast empire from 1960 to 1989, is a passionate music lover, a genuine *mélomane*, as they say in French. He was also a close friend and confidant of the conductor Herbert von Karajan, with whom he would stay in Salzburg, St Moritz and St Tropez, and have endless 'unforgettable' discussions about music and its interpretation. Yet, despite a very successful parallel career as an operatic costumier, Bohan actually tends to prefer symphonic music. 'A great concert satisfies me more deeply and three-dimensionally than an operatic performance, probably because before one can get any degree of real satisfaction in opera, a great many things have to be near-perfect and blend harmoniously with each other: the voices, the orchestra and the conductor, the production, the set and costume designs. It's a lot, you know!'

Bohan was born in 1926 and, in his youth, dreamed of becoming a designer for films rather than fashion, 'because, in those early post-war years, being a couturier was not the glamorous profession we know today; couturiers were not stars, just glorified dress-makers'. In 1945, he joined the house of Robert Piguet, where over four years he learned the couturier's craft. Then followed two years at Molyneux and two at Madeleine de Rauch before in 1954 he became head designer at Jean Patou. He stayed until 1958, when he was appointed head of Dior London, which was creatively independent of its Parisian alma mater. Bohan proved hugely successful in London, and it was there that he developed his own distinctive identity as a fashion designer, honing his modern yet discreet brand of elegance. His clothes were beautifully cut and comfortable to wear, in exquisite fabrics and colours, glamorous without being flamboyant, and always supremely appropriate for whatever occasion they were intended. All good credentials for the stage....

Bohan in fact had his first brush with the theatre during his time at Robert Piguet. The French actor/manager Louis Jouvet, who was staging a production of Molière's play *Don Juan*, approached Piguet to design the costumes. As Piguet later explained to Bohan, he accepted Jouvet's proposal on the sole condition that his young apprentice take full responsibility for the assignment. He himself did not want anything to do with the theatre, 'which is full of crazy people!' 'So,' relates Bohan, 'I had to produce costumes for Donna Elvira – there is no Donna Anna in Molière's play – and I gave her a sublime black dress, as well as a pink and green number, plus two costumes for the peasants, in pastel shades. It was a dream experience for me, and I followed all the rehearsals. But Jouvet felt that the peasants' costumes looked too new, "as if they came straight out of a couture house", and therefore had to be made to look "tired". So, while I suffered agonies inside, someone put them in a bucket in the corridor and squeezed them until they did look pretty tired. Jouvet took one look and exclaimed, "Oh, good, now they look really dirty." When I told Robert Piguet, he replied, "I told you theatre folk are crazy. So we'll charge them even more!" This was a very important first lesson in the difference between costume design and fashion for real life.'

Bohan has also created costumes for countless stars of the silver screen: Sophia Loren in *Arabesque*, Melina Mercouri in films including *Phèdre* (she kept her clothes at the end of shooting), Simone Signoret, Jeanne Moreau, Dominique Sanda and Isabelle Adjani, as well as Marlene Dietrich and Brigitte Bardot both on and off screen. He also regularly dressed Grace Kelly, who became a close friend, after she married Prince Rainier of Monaco. Needless to say, Bohan has numerous stories about his leading ladies. 'Some knew exactly what they wanted and some didn't. Elizabeth Taylor, for instance, had no idea of what she wanted. I once pointed out to her that she needed to have pockets in a particular outfit because, according to the script, in a certain scene she had to put her keys in her pocket. "Oh, you've read the script," she marvelled. "Of course. Haven't you?" I asked in amazement. "Oh, no, I usually cast a quick look at it each morning before shooting."'

Bohan comments, however, that 'designing for films…is exactly the same as designing for real life' and 'a lot less fun than designing for the stage… because there are no rehearsals, and I *love* rehearsals. They are part of the whole experience of designing for the stage, which is a completely different discipline. For a start, a play or an opera is rooted in its own epoch and includes specific characters. A fashion collection, on the other hand, is part of its time, your own time, and not aimed at a specific woman but at women in general; it allows you freedom to follow your fancy. Fashion is a reflection of its time, whereas the theatre is a reflection of a specific story. The costume designer is not free to indulge his own ideas but has to fulfil the director's vision of the story.'

Bohan's first theatrical experience with *Don Juan* was followed by more plays and by early ventures into opera, including Henze's *Boulevard Solitude*, Gluck's *Orfeo ed Euridice*, Ponchielli's *La Gioconda*, Porpora's *Arianna in Nasso*, and Lehár's much-loved operetta, *The Merry Widow*, in a co-production shared by several French opera houses, including Toulon, Nantes, Marseilles, Avignon and Tours. Bohan dressed the eponymous heroine in exquisite, '1950s-style, Ava Gardner-like costumes that suit the plot, as the operetta starts at an embassy ball'. Bohan's mouthwatering evening dresses – which could easily have appeared on the catwalk of a Dior couture collection – stole the show.

One of the landmarks in the designer's career as a costumier was a new production of Mozart's *Don Giovanni* at the Athens Megaron in March 1996. The invitation came from the world-famous bass-baritone Ruggero Raimondi, himself one of the greatest interpreters of the role of Don Giovanni. In this instance, however, Raimondi was not going to be singing; he was going to be directing. The production was the culmination of a project titled 'The Search for Don Giovanni', consisting of an international vocal competition to fill the roles in the opera. The winners would then sing their parts in a production directed by Raimondi, with costumes by Bohan and sets by Giovanni Agostinucci.

'When I accepted Ruggero Raimondi's invitation,' recalls Bohan, 'I proposed Goya as an overall theme and he accepted the idea right away. I had recently seen a Goya

ABOVE Sketch of a costume for Euridice in the Monte Carlo Opera production of Christoph Willibald Gluck's *Orfeo ed Euridice*, 1987. This was one of Marc Bohan's early forays into opera after designing costumes for several plays and dozens of films.

exhibition at the Royal Academy in London, where I realized that the period in which *Don Giovanni* is set coincided with Goya's. Visually, I wanted it to be the complete opposite of Michael Hampe's sombre, black-and-white Salzburg staging [1987]. I wanted a production brimming with the light, sun and colours of Seville, where the opera is set, especially in the scenes with the peasants, whose fiesta should be very sunny and boisterous, exploding with joie de vivre. So all their costumes were in shades of ochre and orange.

'On the other hand, Donna Anna, apart from the nightdress she wears in the opening scene, is always in black, complete with Spanish mantilla and comb, because I felt that black lace is particularly suited to her, as she is a rather "corseted" character – unlike Donna Elvira, who is very pretty and lives life to the full, to say the least, and who therefore had a variety of more colourful costumes. In the last act, for instance, she wore black chiffon, because she is in deep pain, but with lots of bold, gold jewelry, because she is a woman who has tasted and enjoyed life. In the Balcony Scene, she wore a very Goya-esque nightdress in cream lace. But my pride and joy was her costume for her first entry, where she was dressed in a slightly more aggressive manner than usual: a man's habit consisting of a long, Prussian-blue redingote and culottes, topped by a huge, wide-brimmed hat which gives her great allure and perfectly reflects the music at that point, which depicts a very decisive and determined lady. I feel the mannish overtones are also very appropriate dramatically because she is a very daring woman, a woman of spirit, who has crossed half of Spain – from Burgos in the north to Seville in Andalusia – in search of Don Giovanni, the demonic lover who seduced and abandoned her.'

Bohan also enjoyed dressing the men. He tried to liven up the 'rather boring character' of Donna Anna's fiancé, Don Ottavio, by giving him 'a long, grey redingote with epaulettes, which looked great against the backdrop of the soft grey skies of the set'. Naturally, however, 'the most exciting task for any designer of this opera is dressing Don Giovanni himself, this irresistible symbol of male sexuality and potency'. The mere mention of his name instantly conjures up intimate erotic fantasies. Raimondi calls him 'a black hole; a legend who exists only by reflection, through other people's reactions and desires; a legend who dies a spectacular, mythical death so that he can be reborn and renewed constantly, through various authors'. Interpreters of the role must therefore possess considerable stage presence, sex appeal and – according to the late Franco Enriquez, who directed a memorable production at Glyndebourne – a voice that should be not merely beautiful but positively 'spermatozoic'!

In the opening scene, which takes place at night, Bohan wanted Don Giovanni head to toe in black, in thigh-high boots, a waistcoat and a swirling cape, whereas in the scene with the peasants, which takes place in bright sunlight, he dressed him completely in white. 'It seemed obvious that, when everyone else is dressed in shades of orange and ochre, he has to be even more flamboyant. He has to stand out and dazzle at all times.'

For the climax of the opera – the Supper Scene in the finale – Raimondi requested an exceptional costume, something audacious and bizarre. He also wanted it to be able to slip off easily to reveal Don Giovanni's torso. As Raimondi explained, in this scene Don Giovanni provokes God to see if he will respond. This challenge to heaven lies at the crux of the opera and the mystery of Don Giovanni, who cannot, in Raimondi's opinion, be an atheist; he must be a believer who challenges God right up to the end. 'Without this dimension,' he says, 'both the story and the character would lose the grandiose element that makes them so special, and they would become ordinary…because the finale amounts to a duel of titans, in which Don Giovanni is finally overpowered or, rather, removed by extraterrestrial forces, unrepentant and unrelenting to the end. He dies as all legends should – in an extraordinary, mythical way – so that they can go on living.'

Bohan had imagined something more classic for the scene. However, once pointed in this direction and 'because the work is set in Catholic Spain and is about a clash between Good and Evil', he began to imagine something with a religious aspect. 'While at Würzburg Cathedral – one never knows where or when one will find sources of inspiration – I happened to see some statues of the apostles, made of white faience and dressed in gold-embroidered robes. I was so struck by this that I was immediately inspired to create something totally unusual for the Supper Scene, something that would be both aggressive and provocative: a robe, reminiscent of ecclesiastical robes, but in black velvet and full of bold, gold embroidery, shaped not quite like a dressing gown or even a kaftan, but still a garment casual enough for one to wear at home, held together by a chain with a heart that snaps open at a given moment to reveal Don Giovanni's chest.

'In most productions, Don Giovanni is dressed either in red and gold with breeches and waistcoat, or in black, from start to finish. But for a production of this quality – I was always conscious that my director is himself one of the greatest interpreters of the role – I felt one should go further and dare something different. If one dressed Don Giovanni in one of the usual ways, he might still look very handsome and every inch a Grand Seigneur …like so many others. But Don Giovanni is a much more spectacular character – he is a myth – and I feel that dressing him in this great, slightly satanic mantle helps him along on his way to becoming a legend.'

Bohan's designs made such a strong impression that he was invited back to the Athens Megaron in January 1998 to create costumes for a production of Debussy's *Pelléas et Mélisande*, directed by Georg Rootering, with sets by Uwe Belzner and a cast headed by Thomas Allen and Jeannette Pilou. Bohan explained his vision of the characters in this enigmatic opera in the course of a television interview: 'In this very particular work, the psychology and movements of the characters are hugely important. They are not ordinary, everyday characters but strange people who live isolated lives in their castle and inhabit a true psychological "ivory tower". The director and I both felt it crucial to project this seclusion, this alienation from reality, which is an essential part of their natures and inner development. In a sense, although in theory set in the Middle Ages, this opera doesn't belong to any particular period. It is timeless and therefore very modern.'

Bohan noted that he didn't, as a rule, believe in the now fashionable practice of transposing an opera to a different time period from the original conception. 'I do, however, believe in abstracting certain works from their setting and inserting a modern element or insight to make them timeless. Therefore the costumes for this production, about fifteen in all, consist of loose, kaftan-like evening dresses in pastel colours for Mélisande, very classic looks for the men, and a very particular black, woollen, ankle-length dress for [Pelléas's mother] Geneviève, who has surrendered her identity to the castle and is therefore like its prisoner, in a cage. To emphasize this psychological state, I put a long, stiff, black waistcoat over her dress, made of a fabric that looks like a cage.'

When told that he was talking like a director, rather than a costume designer, Bohan replied that, in a sense, a good costume designer *is* a bit of a director, because the costumes play such a crucial part not only in putting the various characters across to the audience, but also in helping the artists themselves to understand their roles – 'which is why it's essential to work in perfect harmony with the director and ensure that you are able to translate his understanding of the work in visual terms, through your costumes'.

OPPOSITE ABOVE Sketch of Don Giovanni's all-black costume for the opening scene in the Athens Megaron production of Mozart's *Don Giovanni*, 1996. As Bohan has noted, the costume 'instantly evokes a Grand Seigneur'.

OPPOSITE BELOW Don Giovanni (Lucas de Jong), wearing a flamboyant white costume in the Athens Megaron production. The scene features peasants dressed in shades of ochre and orange, so Don Giovanni is attired to stand out.

ABOVE Mélisande (Jeannette Pilou) with Pelléas (Thomas Allen) in the Athens Megaron production of Debussy's *Pelléas et Mélisande*, 1998. Bohan designed loose, kaftan-like evening dresses for Mélisande and classic looks for the male characters.

❞ I believe in abstracting certain works from their setting and inserting a modern element or insight to make them timeless.

OPPOSITE The chorus – each member individually dressed – mourns Euridice's death in the Monte Carlo Opera production of Gluck's *Orfeo ed Euridice*, 1987.

ABOVE Euridice (soprano Christine Barbaux) and Orfeo (mezzo Anne Sofie von Otter). The elegant drapery with fine gold details adds dignity to their roles.

RIGHT Euridice (Christine Barbaux) with the chorus, all dressed in Bohan's classically inspired costumes interpreted in a looser, contemporary spirit.

THE MERRY WIDOW

ABOVE LEFT Sketch of a costume for the title character, Hanna Glawari, in the production of Franz Lehár's popular operetta *The Merry Widow* shared between the opera houses of Toulon, Nantes, Marseilles, Avignon and Tours.

ABOVE RIGHT Sketch of a braided uniform for the widow's former love and future husband, Prince Danilo Danilovitsch, First Secretary of the Pontevedrian Embassy.

OPPOSITE Sketch for the ball gown worn by the wealthy widow at the Embassy ball in the opening scene of the operetta.

❝ I dressed the heroine in 1950s-style, Ava Gardner-like costumes that suit the plot, as the operetta starts at an embassy ball.

BELOW Sketches of costumes for the peasants' fiesta. Bohan wanted to capture the light, sun and colours of Seville. His concepts included a dress of apricot-coloured fabric with an apron of white organdie and lace, and a lace-frilled blouse to be worn with a corset.

7

Manches
Munches

8

coiffe 31

Blouse
29
+ Volant
Dentelle

corset
29

Robe 30
Toile abricot

Tablier
organdie Blanc
Dentelle

Tablier
29
Abricot

Jupe
29

OPPOSITE Donna Elvira (Pamela Pantos), wearing a nightdress of cream lace in the Balcony Scene of *Don Giovanni*, staged at the Athens Megaron in 1996. In this scene Donna Elvira is deceived – yet again – by the lothario, who has serenaded her only to get her out of the way in order to seduce her maid.

> **❝** My pride and joy was Donna Elvira's costume for her first entry…a man's habit, topped by a huge, wide-brimmed hat.

OPPOSITE LEFT AND RIGHT Bohan designed a masculine, Prussian-blue redingote and culottes, topped by an alluring hat, for Donna Elvira (sung by Pamela Pantos) in Act I of *Don Giovanni*. The confident costume perfectly matched the music.

LEFT AND ABOVE Bohan's brief was to create a spectacular and provocative costume for Don Giovanni (sung by Lucas de Jong) to wear in the finale of the opera. The gold-embroidered, black velvet robe Bohan created was held together by a chain that could snap open to reveal Don Giovanni's chest.

Christian Lacroix

'Designing for the theatre allows me to breathe'

'I realize that, as a couturier, this is not a very nice thing to say, but I feel that my vibrations are more attuned to opera than to fashion pure and simple,' confided Christian Lacroix when interviewed in 1989 regarding his then new role as a costume designer (for Bizet's *Carmen*). 'Designing for the theatre allows me to breathe.'

Lacroix had burst into prominence two years earlier, with a phantasmagoric landmark collection that put haute couture back on the map and established him as one of the most gifted and original French designers since Yves Saint Laurent. There was certainly more than a whiff of the operatic about his unashamedly seductive and feminine clothes – an explosion of joie de vivre, colour, sensuality and wit, neither conceived nor destined for wallflowers. Indeed, his admirers loved them and his detractors criticized them precisely because they hovered on the borderline between high fashion and costume. This was fully deliberate. According to Lacroix, the borderline is blurred because 'every woman in a couture dress is a sort of diva, an actress, whose outfit expresses who she is, or wishes to be, at that particular moment in time. But in couture there are very few sublime clients! Among them, those who respond to my clothes most strongly and spontaneously, and wear them with the greatest aplomb, are women who are either connected to the theatre in some way or see their clothes as "costumes".'

Surprisingly, Lacroix became a fashion designer more by accident than by intention. After graduating from Montpellier University, where he read Classics and History of Art, and the École du Louvre, where he trained as a museum curator, he began to look for a job and made 'as many appointments with people in the theatre as with people in fashion'. In fact, he showed Pierre Bergé – Yves Saint Laurent's partner, who was then connected to the Théâtre de l'Athénée and later became Director General of the Paris Opera – a dossier of sketches for Puccini's *La Bohème*. Lacroix's main hobby at the time was drawing sets and costumes after every opera he saw, 'because the spectacle on stage usually so dissatisfied or infuriated me that, once back home, I substituted my own designs. But,' he adds somewhat wistfully, 'destiny decided that my career was to be fashion rather than stage design. My first job offer came from the ready-to-wear firm of Guy Paulin, where I stayed for two years, before moving to the haute-couture house of Patou in 1981.' Lacroix stayed at Patou until 1987, when he opened his own couture house in spectacular, whimsically designed premises on the rue Faubourg St Honoré. But although after his first collection he became one of the brightest new stars in the world of fashion, he never let go of his dream of designing for the stage.

His early excursions into costume design were in fact for theatre and ballet. He collaborated on classic plays, including Racine's *Phèdre* and Rostand's *Cyrano de Bergerac* for the Comédie Française (each of which won him a Prix Molière), Alfred de Musset's *Les caprices de Marianne* at the Bouffes du Nord, and Racine's *Bérénice* with Kristin Scott

OPPOSITE Sketch for Carmen's dress in Act IV of Bizet's *Carmen* at the Arènes de Nîmes, 1989. In the finale, Carmen is waiting to watch her current lover, the toreador Escamillo, in a bullfight, when she is stabbed to death by her former lover, Don José.

Thomas at the Avignon Festival and the Théâtre Chaillot in Paris. He also designed ballet costumes for *Tarnished Angels* for Carol Armitage and *Gaîté Parisienne* for Mikhail Baryshnikov and the American Ballet Theatre (both at the Palais Garnier in Paris). In addition he designed the costumes for a famous production of Balanchine's *Jewels* with the Paris Opera Ballet, for which, for the first and only time in his career, he was also in charge of the sets.

He recalls that 'at the beginning, I was not yet taken seriously as a costume designer in the theatre world…just as a fashion designer with aspirations. Some actresses were totally frightened when I first appeared. They thought I was there for a kind of glorified fashion show, confusing the actors with models, without consideration for their personalities or the characters they were about to inter-pret. But the first Prix Molière gave me credibility. Pride, too – a feeling I'm not used to at all. And happiness, of course. And self-confidence.' In fact, these forays into costume design were so successful that Lacroix was invited by director Antoine Bourseiller, a fellow Provençal, to design his first full-length opera – the ever-popular classic, *Carmen*, in an open-air production at the Arènes de Nîmes, a stunning, vast, ancient Roman theatre close to Lacroix's native Arles.

He loved the experience so much that he has continued to design opera on an almost yearly basis, and it has been particu-larly important to him since the untimely closure of his couture house in autumn 2009. He acknowledges that 'my approach was never purely a "fashion" approach; on the contrary, I used stage techniques in order to produce my ideal of couture, since I was always more of a theatrical, operatic designer than a trendsetter or a "streetwear" designer'.

It is no surprise to discover that opera has been Lacroix's consuming passion since boyhood. His love of the genre in general, and *Carmen* in par-ticular, was formed partly by the powerful influence of his maternal grandfather, an opera and bullfighting fanatic, and partly by his birth-place, the city of Arles, positioned both literally and culturally between Italy and Spain, 'exactly between Rome and Madrid'. Lacroix notes that 'for centuries the people there have felt very drawn to these countries. We feel ourselves to be much more "Mediterranean" than French.' Indeed, the designer reckons that the strongest emotions he has ever experienced were at the Italian opera and at the *corrida*. Paradoxically, and he knows this is 'incomprehensible', although in everyday life he cannot bear the sight of blood, he has never been shocked by the sight of a bull's blood, or by this 'choreo-graphy of death between the bulls, which are very sensual, and the *toreros*, those warriors covered in beads, among the most elegant, most sensuous men in the world, and that feminine side of seducing and drawing out the bull…'.

In early childhood, aged two or three, Lacroix would listen with his grand-father to a weekly Sunday lunchtime broadcast of an opera, which to him was

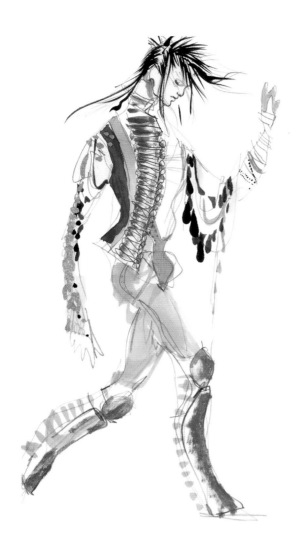

sacred. The signature tune, he remembers, was the trumpet fanfare from the Triumphal March in *Aida*, and the closing tune was the Soldiers' Chorus from *Faust*. That era – the 1950s – was the time of the great rivalry between Maria Callas and Renata Tebaldi, and Lacroix's grandfather was a fierce Tebaldi fan. 'As a child I didn't understand much, but I understood enough to know that there was a war there and felt that I preferred Callas. The dramatic power of her voice, with those sudden leaps from low to high, overwhelmed me, whereas my grandfather thought them horrid!' Indeed, Lacroix declares that he would love to have dressed Callas, both on stage and off.

Another early formative experience was Lacroix's annual attendance of the festival in the Arena, to see operas such as *Carmen*, *Faust* and *Mireille*. He adored those outings. He was 'instantly taken by the magic of it all' and never felt like laughing at those 'fat ladies' in plaits that made up the chorus. 'Even if they were enormous, and the plaits obviously fake, I could instantly make the imaginative link to the story. Then there was the magical Provençal light of the open-air venue, in which one could see the singers arrive and prepare for their entrances.' This passion for opera continued into Lacroix's teens. One of his greatest epiphanies was a production of *Carmen* in the 1950s at the Palais Garnier, with sets and costumes by the legendary Italian stage designer Lila de Nobilis and with wonderful Goya-esque lighting.

Carmen was to retain its hold on Lacroix. To mark the two-hundredth anniversary of the fall of the Bastille, he designed a striking outfit for the mezzo Teresa Berganza (see p. 1). 'I had particularly loved her portrayal of Carmen in Piero Faggioni's production [originally shown at the 1977 Edinburgh Festival], so, when we did this recital dress, I decided it should have overtones of *Carmen*, some of whose music was included in the recital. And I think I can say without false modesty that it was a superb creation, made of flame-coloured silk faille with a big velvet belt and overlaid with gold lace and copper lamé. And for the aria from *Werther*, she had a cape-coat, which she kept for the beginning of Carmen's "Habanera" and played with, swinging it almost like a torero's cape. There

❝ What I like most about working in the theatre is that one cannot be an egoist. It is the director who decides and orders, and I am there to illustrate his imagination.

are very few women like that in couture! I always felt more fulfilled when working with such people, and never more so than when involved in a full operatic production. There is this artistic humility of working as part of a team with the director, the singers, the seamstresses, which I enjoy very much.'

Since his early forays into opera – starting with *Cendrillon* (a work for children, directed in England by Peter Maxwell Davies in 1979) and the famous *Carmen* in Nîmes (1989) – Lacroix has gone on to design an impressive series of productions all over the world, including Charpentier's *Actéon* (2001), Purcell's *Dido and Aeneas* (2001) and Charpentier's *Les Arts florissants* (2004), for William Christie and his ensemble, Les Arts Florissants; Handel's *Theodora* (2002), Mozart's *Il re pastore* (2003), Cavalli's *Eliogabalo*

(2004), Strauss's *Die Frau ohne Schatten* (2005) and Mozart's *Così fan tutte* (2006), for Théâtre Royal de la Monnaie, Brussels; Mozart's *Don Giovanni* (Innsbruck Festival and Baden-Baden, 2006–7), Menotti's *Maria Golovin* (Marseilles, 2006) and Mozart's *Le nozze di Figaro* (Aix en Provence Festival, 2007); Dusapin's *Roméo et Juliette* (2008) and Messager's *Fortunio* (2009), which became a great personal favourite, at the Opéra Comique in Paris; Massenet's *Thaïs* (Metropolitan Opera, New York, 2008–9) and Handel's *Agrippina* (Berlin State Opera, 2010). Most of these were conducted by René Jacobs and directed by Vincent Boussard, who, along with the director Denis Podalydès, has become a close friend of Lacroix's.

With so much experience of both the fashion and the operatic world, Lacroix is ideally placed to explain the differences between the two and how they can be bridged. 'The biggest difference is that in fashion – both in the concept of a collection and its presentation to the public – the designer is the absolute boss, whereas in stage design the opposite is true. What I like most about working in the theatre is that one cannot be an egoist. It is the director of the production who decides and orders, and I am there to illustrate his imagination. Sometimes it's very precise, both in terms of shapes and colours, and sometimes it's much freer. But my pleasure and satisfaction lie in sketching according to the director's wish. But, at the same time, I also need to be fair and true to myself, by feeling and experiencing the work at hand very deeply and as coherently as possible with my own style, approach and sense of pleasure. This implies the existence of total chemistry, or alchemy, between the piece, the director and myself. If this kind of rapport doesn't exist, no way would I do it! But if it does, then I will listen to the director's concept and view of the piece in hours and hours of briefings. As far as the sets are concerned, the set designer is usually a very close collaborator of the director's, so my friends' friends are my friends, too…and working to the same mood is easy. It's really a matter of teamwork. This is why I'm very cautious before agreeing to work on a project.'

Once the initial rapport and collaborative basis have been established, Lacroix needs to know who the singers will be. 'Naturally I can't start sketching before having their figure and style in mind; without seeing a photo with measurements. Then I follow my instinct and inspiration, my first feelings for the piece, through a series of sketches which I propose to the director – sometimes this may involve a lot of images in order to translate my vision more precisely – before starting, with the director's okay, on final maquettes.'

This approach is confirmed by Vincent Boussard, who points out that 'Christian is rare in that he places himself at the service of the piece, the director's concept and the team in general, with extreme modesty. He listens very carefully at preparatory meetings, takes kilometres of notes and then disappears for quite some time. Then he reappears with masses of sketches – some of which are in accordance with my concept, and some not – for me to choose.'

In terms of style, Lacroix likes mixing costumes inspired by the period when the opera in question was composed, with some contemporary touches,

and, where applicable, designs relevant to the period in which the action of the story is actually set. He deplores the fact that more and more directors are less and less fond of period costumes.

He is observant of the ways in which fashion and costume design differ conceptually and technically. 'A couture dress is conceived and made to be seen at close quarters, whereas a theatrical or operatic costume must be clearly visible and make an impact from afar. Close to, it can be as ugly as you like! What brought this point home to me with a loud bang were the sensational costumes for *Salome* by a Romanian designer. They were made out of the kind of plastic used for bin bags, but, processed in a way that from a distance made them shimmer beguilingly, they instantly created a magical atmosphere, even though at close quarters they were hideously vulgar. That is what theatre is all about, and it was a very important lesson for me. At a pinch, I would say that my *Carmen* costumes for Nîmes were too couture-like, too nuanced, almost good enough for real life. But what Bourseiller wanted was an almost contemporary *Carmen*, with resonances of the Spanish Civil War, and he chose me because the entire production team consisted of a band of people from the Midi, almost like a club.'

As it happened, the Nîmes Arena had spent a fortune on the previous season's production of *Attila* and was so short of money that Lacroix's budget for *Carmen* was nearly zero. Yet, although he complained bitterly, this seems to have acted as a stimulus for him to be even more original and creative. He found most of the fabrics and accessories at the Rastro, Madrid's open-air market, 'where, among a lot of rubbish, you can find some splendid paisley, cashmere and antique brocade shawls, lace tablecloths, embroidered sheets and napkins', which is what most of the costumes for the Cigarette Girls were made of, with the addition of some crochet and lace blouses, 'all done with very little money'. Carmen's stunning Act IV dress was made out of an antique curtain decorated with embroideries and passementeries, also found in Madrid.

The other costumes were equally memorable. Lacroix recalls with amusement the outfit he designed for Escamillo, 'a big Texan guy for whom we made a real torero costume. Now, dressing a torero before a corrida is quite a ritual and requires a valet or special dresser, who has to put his hand inside the torero's trousers in order to pull them tightly into place. But this rather puritanical Texan gentleman greatly objected to this custom and made quite a scene!' The costume for the character of Micaëla was, according to Lacroix, 'very *jeune fille de bonne famille très bien élevée* and consisted of a matelassé skirt, a white blouse with lace sleeves, and a little jacket with passementeries – an echo of the costumes I used to see at the Fête in Arles, where people used to sing in Provençal'. The smugglers' ponchos were army blankets, treated with cotton string. Lacroix also rented hundreds of capes, which were then decorated with multicoloured patchwork (this was eventually removed and the capes returned). All the costumes were made by hand in outdoor workshops in Nîmes, supervised by an English assistant, who had worked with the great French theatre director Ariane Mnouchkine and lived nearby. The local seamstresses entered into this game of improvisation with gusto and dedication. 'The atmosphere was fantastic,' recalls Lacroix. 'We had great fun.'

His passion for *Carmen* was further conditioned by what he describes as his 'first emotional awareness of sensuality, which hit me like a gale force when, as a small child, I first saw a gypsy, half naked, hypnotically absorbed in a dance, her skin glowing with a dark sheen.… I have always carried this image inside me. At the time, whenever I was taken for a walk by my grandmother, I insisted that we went past the gypsy camp. *Petit bourgeois* child that I was, I felt deeply drawn to these families I saw going away in their caravans, and fascinated by the women and children who had no ties and were free to roam the world. I dreamed of going away with them. Even though I was frightened by old wives' tales about gypsies stealing children, secretly I longed to be stolen.… So my image of Carmen is of an archetypal gypsy – sensual, mysterious and *free*! There is something almost Verdian in the way she sings "*la liberté, la liberté*", something tremendously powerful. Like Don Giovanni, she would rather die than lose her freedom. I see Don Giovanni as Carmen's twin. Both die for the right to live as they please and do what they like. That is why these two characters are legends. Nobody ever possessed them.'

❝ I loved Renée Fleming's openness, her fantasy, her frankness, her rigour, her interest in the costumes, and her lucidity about herself.

Lacroix went on to design the costumes for Vincent Boussard's production of *Don Giovanni*, conducted by René Jacobs, at the Innsbruck Festival in 2006 and Baden-Baden in 2007. The production was interesting because Boussard and Jacobs deliberately took the work back to its eighteenth-century origins, both musically and dramatically. Lacroix accordingly designed a beautiful set of period costumes that were at the same time very modern. For Don Giovanni in the finale, he created a long gold and blue striped coat, lined in red, with colourful details such as a collar trimmed in pink and a yellow gilet, combined with camouflage-type printed trousers that allowed the singer to run around the stage with élan.

While Lacroix was fully satisfied with his work for *Don Giovanni*, he states that he would one day like to design another *Carmen*. In fact, he has a second *Carmen* dossier ready, because at the time of the first production he had presented Antoine Bourseiller with two alternatives. 'In the first one, Carmen was much more sulphuric, Goya-esque and resonant of the shapes and colours of the 1890s, with echoes of 1814.' Much to Lacroix's disappointment, Bourseiller chose the second version, in which Carmen had a much more fluid silhouette, inspired by the 1930s. Despite having to renounce his own preference, Lacroix once again remained equanimous.

His humility is confirmed by John Cox, who directed the Metropolitan Opera's production of *Thaïs* in 2009, simultaneously screened live in over 850 cinemas worldwide. 'As a colleague and collaborator, Christian was utterly charming, very attentive, not at all self-assertive, totally unlike a fashion designer. He understands theatre.' Initially, Cox had been far from pleased to have Lacroix thrust upon him as a costume designer for this production, which had already been seen at the Chicago Lyric Opera with costumes by the distinguished operatic costume designer Paul Brown and sets by Mauro Pagano. However, one of the world's greatest sopranos, Renée Fleming, was to sing the title role, and she had

BELOW Athanaël (Thomas Hampson) and Thaïs (Renée Fleming) in Act I of Jules Massenet's *Thaïs* at the Metropolitan Opera, New York, 2009. The production, directed by John Cox, was screened live in HD to 868 cinemas worldwide, as part of the Met's annual 'Live from the Met' series.

decided she wanted costumes specially designed by Lacroix – who, along with John Galliano and Karl Lagerfeld, had designed the costumes for the three heroines whose music she had sung at her gala recital at the opening of the 2008–9 season.

Peter Gelb, the inspirational General Manager of the Metropolitan Opera, was the person responsible for inviting the three designers to create the costumes for the gala, an event – featuring acts from *La traviata*, *Manon* and *Capriccio* – that had been scheduled prior to his appointment at the Met. 'Each of the designers worked at cost,' he reports, 'and each was sent videos and photographs of the productions so that they could take into account the characters in each opera and the overall stage design, in so far as the technicalities were concerned. There were some complications, as fittings had to take place in Europe to fit into the designers' schedules. There was more coaching than usual from our in-house design team to make sure that the practicalities of function were dealt with – like making sure that Renée would be able to move freely around the stage, that sort of thing.'

Lacroix's costume, which was for *La traviata* – 'a vast tea gown, a little Beaton-esque…in rather melancholy pastels, with antique feather flowers scattered across the bodice' – was Fleming's favourite, hence her decision that he should design the costumes for *Thaïs*. Cox was 'sort of informed' about this decision. However, despite being highly sceptical of the 'vanity project', he went to Paris, met Lacroix and had a lengthy and constructive conversation with him. Lacroix, a true professional, had spread an entire portfolio of designs over a long cutting table in his studio to show Cox. Some were new and some had already been sent to Fleming, who had indicated which ones she liked and which she didn't. Lacroix's chief cutter was already travelling all over the world, to wherever she was performing, 'so Christian was a bit wiser about how to deal with the situation. We had a very good working conversation, during which I was able to show him the Chicago scenery and costumes and talk about how they were lit and so on, things that he didn't know. Together we settled on some costume designs that were absolutely stunning, and were beautifully lit and filmed for the live relay.' Lacroix emerged from this collaboration totally satisfied and as enthusiastic about his diva as she was about him: 'I loved her openness, her fantasy, her frankness, her rigour, her interest in the costumes, and her lucidity about herself.'

Since then, Lacroix's most important assignment has been Handel's *Agrippina* for the Berlin State Opera, directed by Boussard, who points out that ten years had passed since the two had worked together on another Handel opera, *Theodora*, 'which is totally different, almost an oratorio, whereas *Agrippina* is Handel's most "Italian" opera, a very dramatic work, full of very strong characters. We had great singers, and Christian and I worked with tremendous creative freedom. I wanted to create a Rome that has echoes and resonates with today's public. The opera is about power and its exercise – over people on the personal level, and peoples in the political sense. This pursuit and manipulation of power are not confined to any period. They are timeless and universal. Christian surpassed himself. His costumes were brilliant. He has a modern perception of things, which he works and blends, intuitively, with historical references.' Lacroix names this production as one

of the most memorable and exciting of his career, on both an artistic and personal level, and for the total degree of harmony that existed among the creative team. 'It was a wonderful experience to work with former East German workrooms,' he says. '*Agrippina* was a fantastic success that has brought interesting new propositions.'

These include productions of Leonard Bernstein's *Candide* in Berlin, Bellini's *I Capuleti ed I Montecchi* at the Bavarian State Opera in Munich, another production of

〝*Agrippina* has been one of the most memorable and exciting productions of my career.

Carmen with Vincent Boussard in Stockholm (it will be interesting to see if Lacroix persuades Boussard to use his alternative *Carmen* dossier), Verdi's *Aida* in Cologne, and Donizetti's *Don Pasquale* at the Théâtre des Champs-Elysées with Denis Podalydès. Lacroix – who may now become a full-time theatrical costumier – is particularly thrilled that these plans include his first Verdi opera. He also longs to design *Il trovatore*, which has been one of his favourite works since he was a teenager. He would also like to work on a Puccini production, especially *La Bohème* and *Madama Butterfly*.

This supremely talented, modest and likeable man certainly brings a unique combination of gifts to costume design – his innate theatricality, which is never there for its own sake but always in order to illuminate the characters and the truth of the work at hand; a profound academic knowledge of history and period costume; and, last but not least, an unparalleled, exuberant visual imagination.

OPPOSITE Sketch of a costume for Poppea in Handel's *Agrippina* at the Berlin State Opera, 2010. The design was prophetic, from a fashion point of view, in that it prefigured a major trend of the autumn/winter 2010 collections: 1950s-style, waisted, wide skirts, dresses and coats.

ABOVE Christian Lacroix with exhibits from a major exhibition of his work for the stage at the Paris Opera's Palais Garnier, 2006.

OVERLEAF Sketches of gypsies' costumes for Antoine Bourseiller's production of Bizet's *Carmen* at the Arènes de Nîmes, 1989.

CARMEN

... seen (opposite) toasting each other in the open-air Arènes de Nîmes. The costumes were largely made from materials found by Lacroix at the Rastro, Madrid's largest street market.

" In the Rastro you can find some splendid paisley, cashmere and antique brocade shawls, lace tablecloths, embroidered sheets and napkins.

❝ The "hands" in the workrooms of each opera house are terribly important. I focus on the particular skills of each one, their talents for dyeing and painting, of finding subtle ways of adding eighteenth-century touches to costumes.

LEFT AND ABOVE Sketches for Tamiri and Aminta in Mozart's comparatively rarely produced early opera, *Il re pastore*, for the Théâtre Royal de la Monnaie in Brussels, 2003. This marked one of Lacroix's first collaborations with the director Vincent Boussard, and the first of many with La Monnaie.

OPPOSITE Aminta, the shepherd king (Annette Dasch), and Tamiri, his shepherdess lover (Raffaella Milanesi). With this opera, Lacroix and Vincent Boussard started to explore ways of expressing the eighteenth century with a youthful modernity and a lightness of touch.

Atilia

manches transparentes amovibles

corselet taille haute

ceinture taille basse

> The costumes for most of the characters in *Eliogabalo* were an almost cartoonesque extravaganza, inspired by the carnivals of Cavalli's eighteenth century.

ABOVE Sketch for the Roman beauty, Atilia. The director Vincent Boussard had admired Lacroix's couture collection of the previous season and asked the designer to use the fashion show finale to inspire gowns for the female characters in the production of *Eliogabalo* staged at the Théâtre Royal de la Monnaie in Brussels, 2004.

OPPOSITE ABOVE AND BELOW Sketches for Lenia, the nanny of the boy emperor Eliogabalo. Lacroix enjoyed experimenting with old fabrics left in storage and pieces of damaged embroidery to evoke glamour and opulence with humble materials.

RIGHT Sketch for Don Alfonso in Mozart's *Così fan tutte* at the Théâtre Royal de la Monnaie in Brussels, 2006, Lacroix's second encounter with Mozart.

BELOW Sketch for Fiordiligi. The libretto imagines the two sisters in *Così fan tutte* as teenagers. Although the singing cast are naturally more mature, Lacroix nonetheless played with lingerie-like transparencies for their costumes.

TOP AND ABOVE Costumes for characters, including Ferrando (sung by Pavol Breslik) and Fiordiligi (Virginia Tola). Lacroix and Vincent Boussard sought a modern, pure, abstract expression of the eighteenth century.

55

Così

soldat

velours

son
lady

got
fol

Guglielmo
&
Ferrando

OPPOSITE Sketch for Dorabella, the more
sensual of the two sisters in *Così fan tutte*.
For her costumes Lacroix made much use
of drawstrings and crepeline, a light chiffon
usually used for restoring antique fabrics.

RIGHT Sketch for the soldier's uniform that
both Guglielmo and Ferrando wear at the
beginning and the finale of the opera.

66 My choice of colour for
Agrippina's costumes would
have been a brownish red,
the colour of dried blood,
but Vincent Boussard, the
director, didn't like the idea, so
most of the time she tends to
wear very couture-like black.

PREVIOUS PAGES A dramatic shot of Ottone
(Bejun Mehta) in Handel's *Agrippina*
at the Berlin State Opera, 2010. The
production was so successful that it led
to invitations to five other German opera
houses, and one Swedish, for the
Boussard/Lacroix team.

ABOVE Nerone (Jennifer Rivera), Agrippina
(Alexandrina Pendatchanska) and Pallante
(Neal Davies) in a modern setting chosen
to reflect the exercise of power.

OPPOSITE ABOVE AND BELOW Agrippina (sung
by Alexandrina Pendatchanska), with
(below) her freeman Pallante (Neal
Davies). Their striking accessories and
make-up offset the 'couture-like black'.

LEFT Sketch showing structured tailoring with a bold outline, though in the end the director, Vincent Boussard, preferred black for Agrippina's costumes.

❝ The pursuit and manipulation of power are not confined to any place or period. They are timeless and universal.

VINCENT BOUSSARD, DIRECTOR

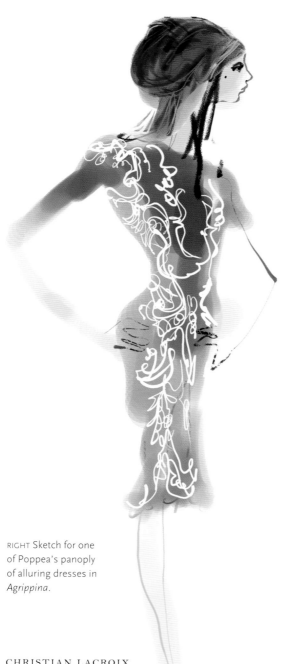

RIGHT Sketch for one of Poppea's panoply of alluring dresses in *Agrippina*.

CENTRE AND LEFT The scheming
seductress Poppea (sung by
Anna Prohaska), seen here in
a lavish costume with a long
train. Poppea overcomes the
plots and power games of
Agrippina, Emperor Nero's
equally scheming mother, and
wins the emperor's heart and
the throne of Rome.

Karl Lagerfeld

'I adore doing opera. I know the history of opera by heart. I know my classical composers.'

It is perhaps not surprising that Karl Lagerfeld should love the opera; nor that, with his costumes for Offenbach's *Les Contes d'Hoffmann* at the Maggio Musicale Fiorentino in 1980, he should have been one of the pioneers leading the way for fashion designers to step onto the operatic stage. Lagerfeld – the architect of the resurrection of the house of Chanel, the designer who revolutionized the conceptual and technical approach to fur as head designer at Fendi, while simultaneously heading up Chloe and designing for his own label, and becoming an accomplished photographer along the way – is, after all, a profoundly cultured, astonishingly well-read polymath, a scintillating, polyglot conversationalist and a restless, adventurous spirit perpetually in search of new challenges. Like the cream of the profound and brilliant, he has the gift of appearing tantalizingly superficial, given to dishing out maxims and delightful *bons mots* (known in the fashion world as Karlisms) at the speed of light – the speed to which his inner clock is permanently set – but the surprise lies in the staggering breadth and depth of his knowledge of the operatic genre, its history and its performers both past and present.

'I adore doing opera,' he exclaims, when alerted to the fact that he was one of the first fashion designers to cross the floorboards of the operatic *palcoscenico*. But he adds that he does not think the link between fashion and opera is all that new, despite the fact that on the whole designers were not directly involved in opera until recently. 'In the early decades of the twentieth century, the 1920s and 1930s,' he says, 'the costumes of singers such as Lotte Lehmann or Germaine Lubin were very influenced by the fashions of the day, so there has always been an indirect, cyclical interplay between the two.'

The happiest of all Lagerfeld's experiences of working in opera was *Les Contes d'Hoffmann*, which, together with *Les Troyens*, was directed by the distinguished Italian director Luca Ronconi, with whom Lagerfeld had earlier collaborated on several plays, including Hugo von Hoffmansthal's *Der Schwierige* in Salzburg (Lagerfeld also designed costumes at the Burgtheater in Vienna for a previously unstaged play by Arthur Schnitzler, directed by the erstwhile artistic director of the Salzburg Festival, Jürgen Flimm). Of *Les Contes d'Hoffmann*, he says: 'Everyone – Ronconi, the conductor Antonio de Almeida, the set designer Jean-Paul Chambas – was in total harmony, and we had great singers: Brigitte Fassbaender, who was fabulous as Giulietta, Catherine Malfitano as Antonia, the wonderful late Sesto Bruscantini as the four villains, and a young American with a very pretty voice, Arleen Auger, as the doll, Olympia. I loved that work and stayed in Florence for a long time because I was enjoying myself so much. My favourite of the opera's three heroines is the courtesan, Giulietta. And I am mad about the "Barcarolle", at the beginning and end of her act, which is somewhat kitsch but gorgeous and very melancholy, like the waltz in *Der Rosenkavalier*. There is nothing more melancholy than the waltz in *Der Rosenkavalier*, which I adore. Three notes and one is off!' (A propos of

OPPOSITE Sketch of an all-white costume to be worn by Norma, High Priestess of the Celts, with bold jewelry and a wide bronze-coloured belt, in the Monte Carlo Opera production of Bellini's *Norma*, 2009.

waltzes, it should be noted that Lagerfeld once hosted waltz and tango evenings in the enormous ground-floor ballroom of his former home in the Rue de l'Université. He says he can 'still dance very well' and proudly shows off his new, eccentrically different 'ballroom' – a vast, book-lined space, which also serves as his photographic studio, at the back of the Lagerfeld Gallery in Rue de Lille.)

It was Ronconi's idea to invite a couturier to design his production of *Les Contes d'Hoffmann*: 'I have always thought it a very good idea to ask a fashion designer to do costumes in opera because they bring a rather innovative spirit to the work.' Ronconi himself convinced Lagerfeld to take the leap…'which was all very well,' recalls Lagerfeld, 'but when I came to do the costumes I discovered that you should never have them made in a couture house, as I had done. It never works. When I was confronted on stage by those perfectly made and finished couture dresses, they all looked paltry and anaemic, as if they didn't quite make the grade. So I redesigned everything again, on the spot. It was not a question of changing my conception but the approach to its realization – doing the same designs in different fabrics; making a broad-brush statement of the same concept – because a couture house is trained to execute a dress with minute attention to every tiny detail, which has to be perfect…all of which is totally wasted on stage. Here you need costumes that make a splash from afar. At close quarters they can look as imperfect as you like. For this reason you have to use different materials. No point in going for the softest, finest, most delicate silks; the effect gets lost in the distance. And your satins don't have to be the best in the world; they can easily be synthetic. Something of inferior quality but with a shiny finish will look far more effective. The stage acts as an amplifier and you have to make bold statements.'

Lagerfeld points out that designing costumes for the cinema is a very different matter. 'Cinema is more real than reality itself, because you see everything close up. So every detail must be done perfectly. For instance, on film, for every back view of a dress, we ensure there is no zip or any kind of fastening. But of course this means doing two dresses, one for the front and one for the back view, which is very expensive. I am the only one who still does that. When you see most Hollywood films, you always see zips or buttons at the back. So in cinema detail is everything, whereas opera is quite the opposite.'

Lagerfeld's second venture onto the operatic stage, *Les Troyens* at La Scala in 1982, was somewhat less enjoyable than *Hoffmann*, although he was pleased with his costumes, which, indeed, were spectacularly evocative. There were difficulties with the stage designer, who was used to working in partnership with his wife as a set/costume design duo, and was disappointed not to be doing so in this case. In addition, Lagerfeld found the experience of working at La Scala 'a nightmare, because the place was completely dominated by the unions and their stupid rules! For example, we couldn't go to the canteen for a cup of coffee, because we didn't belong to the local union, and had to go to the bistro across the street. And the orchestra seemed to feel they were entitled to a pause almost every five minutes. I thought the conductor, Georges Prêtre, would murder them!' In this particular production, Prêtre did not feature the ballets that Berlioz had included in Act IV. Lagerfeld comments: 'Ballet is always an indispensable part of French opera, and even composers like Verdi inserted ballets into their operas for their French airings. But then the opera was revived in 1996 and the new conductor, Colin Davis, a renowned champion of Berlioz, did include it, and I produced extra costumes.'

❝ If you hear earlier singers, such as Frida Leider or Kirsten Flagstad, there is no screaming. They had sweet voices, unlike today's Wagnerians, whose aim is to shatter glass!

Lagerfeld's third foray into opera was Puccini's charming work, *La Rondine* ['The Swallow'], in 1992, at the Monte Carlo Opera, where the work had had its world premiere in 1917. Lagerfeld loves Puccini – 'not *Turandot* with all that chinoiserie, or *La fanciulla del West* with its Wild West Americana' – but *Tosca*, *Manon Lescaut*, *Madama Butterfly* and, of course, *La Rondine*, for which he produced poetic, atmospheric costumes that enhanced the charm and poignant lightness of touch so characteristic of the work, which Puccini had originally conceived as an operetta for Vienna. Nelly Miricioiu, who sang the heroine Magda, found the experience of working with Lagerfeld 'phenomenal'. 'He was extremely nice to everybody. One never heard a cross word. He followed everything that was going on on stage. When we did the fittings, he would move and flit from one to the other with the speed of lightning and could instantly spot any fault or problem in any of our costumes, which absolutely reflected the characters. In fact, each character was already *in* the costume! He loved the music, and connected with and understood exactly what we were doing. Just stepping into my costume gave me the character's personality. His striped coat was shaped exactly like a swallow, mirroring the title of the opera. The black dress was intended to convey the "matrona", while the pink, embroidered dress represented Magda's happiness; *la vie en rose*! I was four months pregnant at the time, but certainly didn't look it in his costumes. He was nice enough to say that I moved better than a model. And at the premiere he sent me the hugest, most gorgeous arrangement of white flowers I have ever seen.' (Provided you don't cross him, Lagerfeld is indeed extremely pleasant, courteous and sensitive, but he finds his reputation to the contrary amusing and occasionally useful. 'Apparently I am very frightening. But if people get to know me a little, they will find that I am a very nice, down-to-earth person. But, thank God, I don't look like one.') Miricioiu adds that, 'personal memories apart, I think that perhaps the most remarkable thing about his costumes was that when you came to the show, you didn't think, "Oh, these are so Karl Lagerfeld." You thought of the story. And I think this was very humble of him and showed his artistic integrity.'

When asked if designing costumes for the opera is a very different discipline from designing for couture, Lagerfeld replies with a little hesitation. 'I wouldn't say so. Not necessarily. It depends on the director and his concept.' He notes that he would absolutely refuse to work with a director whose concept involved putting characters in modern costume. 'I hate that,' he states, 'especially in Mozart's operas, or the great Italian romantic works, or one of Richard Strauss's "Viennese" operas, which I would love to design costumes for. But not *Die Frau ohne Schatten*, definitely not for me, with that nagging Dyer's Wife and whatnot. Not very amusing, is it? Russian opera isn't my cup of tea either. Korngold's *Die tote Stadt* would be quite interesting. French opera I am in two minds about, apart from the two I have designed, that is: *Les Contes d' Hoffmann* – and *Les Troyens*, which is sublime and without doubt the greatest French opera.'

The opera he would most like to design for is Strauss's *Der Rosenkavalier,* not least because it is set in the eighteenth century, a period for which Lagerfeld feels a particular affinity, to the extent of amassing a huge collection of priceless eighteenth-century paintings and furniture. 'I adore *Der Rosenkavalier*,' he says, 'and know it by heart. The greatest Marschallin was the first, Lotte Lehmann. Next to her everyone pales. She was unique and, like many of the great singers of her time, she had a very sweet, creamy voice, something which seems to have vanished in our day, at least in the heavier German repertoire. Since Birgit Nilsson became the foremost Wagnerian soprano of the day – and by the way, no, I am not interested in designing for a Wagnerian opera – everybody screams. But if you hear earlier singers, such as Frida Leider or Kirsten Flagstad, there is no screaming. They had sweet voices, unlike today's Wagnerians, whose aim is to shatter glass! Callas, on the other hand, even when she sings with a piercing sound, is always thrilling and remains the very incarnation of Italian melodrama. I saw her in *Tosca* five times and can never forget her. I don't feel like seeing another *Tosca*, or *La sonnambula*, or *I Puritani*, or *Norma*, in my life *ever*. Even though I designed costumes for *Norma* in Monte Carlo, there is no one alive who could come close to Callas in that role. There was mystery, there was another dimension, to her performances. It goes without saying that I would have loved to design costumes for her. I never saw her in Donizetti's *Lucia*, an opera I also adore, but just a bit less than Bellini's *I Puritani*, which has a happier ending. But after its Paris premiere, on 25 January 1835, with four great singers – Grisi, Lablache, Tamburini and Rubini – it was not as big a success in Italy, because it requires four great voices, unlike *Lucia*, where you can make do with three. I also love *Capriccio* and saw Elisabeth Schwarzkopf singing the final monologue in concert.'

Would Lagerfeld agree that he is quite the opera connoisseur? 'Oh yes, oh yes, oh yes. I know the history of opera by heart. I know my classical composers. One of my most favourite is Bellini. I love *belcanto*, Bellini, Donizetti, but especially Bellini. He is my number one favourite. I don't think anyone has ever written as beautifully for the human voice as Bellini, in *I Puritani*, *La sonnambula*, which was written for Maria Malibran, and *Norma* for Giuditta Pasta. I also like Rossini, not just *Barbiere* but especially Rossini *serio* – *Tancredi* and *La donna del lago*.'

If he had time, which he does not, he would only be tempted to return to designing for the operatic stage either in the Strauss operas mentioned or in the *belcanto* repertoire: '*Lucia*, or better still *I Puritani*, which is very Van Dyke. But not with a director who might opt to have the Cavaliers or Cromwell's Puritans dressed as Nazis! Not that! I hate what is called "director's opera". Opera lives through singers. Without singers, it's nothing. If you approach opera too realistically, it doesn't work, in my opinion. Opera must remain in the sphere of dreams…. If you impose modernity on opera, it often clashes with the music. But, as far as the future is concerned, I think that opera as a genre has a problem in that the most beautiful operas – from Monteverdi to our own day – have already been written. There is Henze's *Elegie für junge Liebende* [Elegy for Young Lovers, 1961], but otherwise….'

OPPOSITE Sketch of a costume for Hoffmann (sung by Neil Shicoff), sporting an earring on his visit to Giulietta in the Venice Scene of Jacques Offenbach's *Les Contes d'Hoffmann* at the Teatro Comunale in Florence, 1980. Offenbach's centenary year also saw important productions of the work at the Salzburg Festival and Covent Garden.

ABOVE Sketch of a grey velvet jacket and lilac-pink velvet waistcoat for Dapperutto, the last of the four villains (sung by Sesto Bruscantini) in *Les Contes d'Hoffmann*.

ABOVE Sketch for Norma's father, Oroveso, the High Priest, in the Monte Carlo Opera production of *Norma*.

OPPOSITE Sketch for the young priestess Adalgisa in the Monte Carlo Opera production of *Norma*.

Does he have any favourites among today's divas? 'Are there any? They certainly don't seem to grow on trees. I liked the lady for whom I designed the costume for *Manon*, Renée Fleming…although I prefer Puccini's *Manon Lescaut* to Massenet's *Manon*, especially that aria at the beginning of Act II, where she arrives and is impatient, and which Callas sang to perfection. I never saw her sing this role on stage, nor Lucia, which I would have loved, but I did see it with Joan Sutherland, who was also a great singer.' Male favourites include 'Ruggero Raimondi, who sadly doesn't sing much anymore, and Placido Domingo, whom I last saw at his Operalia vocal contest in Paris a few years back. I adore competitions, simply adore them. I also find them very interesting. Mind you, nowadays almost all the contestants seem to be Chinese or Korean, which is admirable, the way they have mastered an art form totally alien to their own traditions.' Of favourite conductors, Lagerfeld exclaims, 'Undoubtedly Furtwängler! Not only the greatest of conductors, but also a highly cultured man, which most of them used to be, in those days….'

It must be obvious by now that keeping Karl Lagerfeld focused on talking about a single topic for longer than a few minutes is well nigh impossible. Nonetheless, his amusing forthrightness is instructive. When asked if he thinks one of the reasons why so many designers are branching into opera is connected to the fact that fashion is now so closely related to 'showbiz', with collections presented as 'spectacles' of clothes, some of which are not only never sold but not even manufactured, he snorts, 'Not everybody does that! What is the point of making clothes knowingly intending them never to be worn? I call that runway masturbation! We are all in the business of making and selling clothes to real women. Clothes that go into a museum without being worn, I am very much against. The other day I asked a fellow designer what he was up to at the moment and he replied that he was "making art". So I said, "What? Have you stopped designing dresses?" Because all that rigmarole about us couturiers being artists is nonsense. We are not artists; we are merchants.'

Although the iconic image Lagerfeld has created for himself is romantic and reminiscent of an eighteenth-century operatic character – the silver ponytail, the high starched shirt collar, the impeccably cut suits, and, in earlier years, the ubiquitous fan – he is very pragmatic and focused on today and tomorrow. Aware of everything going on in every field, from technology to pop, and always reinventing himself and expanding his creative output, he says, 'I never bother about what I have done before. I *do*. I am all for doing, not for having done!'

His own life and career have certainly been fascinating. He was born into an affluent, cultured family in Schleswig-Holstein, but grew up near Hamburg, with a father who was the owner of a condensed milk company that he sold to Carnation. His father was Swedish on his own father's side and Polish on his mother's, and the latter was perhaps the reason why he converted to Catholicism – 'he and my grandmother were hysterical Catholics' – and was rejected by his strictly Protestant Swedish family. Lagerfeld's mother, who lived in his château in Brittany until her death in 1978, was a dominant influence in his life. She decided that her son – his parents' favourite, a fact apparently stoically accepted by his two sisters – should grow up without any religion. 'A gypsy had told my mother that I would become a priest, and she became so alarmed, and so detested the idea – and that of my becoming a dancer – that she ensured I never set foot in a church, not for a wedding, a christening, a funeral, nothing, probably out of fear that I might be seduced by that world.' (She may also have noted that the young Karl, a clothesaholic from as far back as he can remember, had apparently expressed great admiration for cardinals' robes.)

Lagerfeld's passion for clothes was spotted and encouraged by his family very early on, and, when he demanded it, he was given a valet at the age of four, 'so that I could have clean clothes after my siesta. My father thought it was important to be well dressed, and my mother changed four times a day. As for myself, I have always loved clothes passionately.' Today he has a vast collection of shirts, all from the Paris branch of Hilditch & Key. He claims to be their biggest client, saying they have produced more than three hundred shirts for him over the years. Would he call himself a shirt fetishist, then? 'No. But certainly a shirt freak!' He also loves packing. 'I love touching and caressing my clothes. I travel with ten suitcases, even when going away just for a week, because on top of the clothes there are all the books, and the stationery, for which I also have a passion. I am a paper freak, mad about stationery. It's a physical pleasure.' (He tends to write his letters himself, by hand.) 'But all that luggage is why I don't like to travel anymore.'

OVERLEAF LEFT Sketch for the all-white costume worn by the doll, Olympia, in *Les Contes d'Hoffmann*. Only the face and hands are exposed, emphasizing the 'artificial' aspect, though a note adds that white gloves may also be added.

OVERLEAF RIGHT Sketch for the courtesan Giulietta in *Les Contes d'Hoffmann*, featuring a wrap trimmed with bands of fur and lines of pearls.

❝ I never bother about what I have done before. I *do*. I am all for doing, not for having done!

He mastered French and English while still a child. Constantly avid for new experiences, he moved to Paris in his late teens and started his life in fashion as an apprentice in Pierre Balmain's famous couture house. But he says, 'fashion in the 1950s was like the Third World of today. We just worked and worked, while Balmain took the money, and we were left to starve in the back room and were paid nothing.' In 1959, he moved to Patou. Then from 1965 he designed for Chloe, the ready-to-wear firm that he elevated to unprecedented heights, especially in the late 1960s and 1970s. He left in 1983, the year he was appointed design director at Chanel. The rest is history....

Lagerfeld has always been employed on a freelance basis and has never involved himself with the business side of any of the firms with which he has been associated. When he signed up with Chanel, he reportedly managed to secure an annual salary of over a million dollars. An immensely generous friend, who often gives exquisite and precious gifts to his friends and muses, he has also been a prolific collector throughout his life. In the late 1990s, however, he sold his château in Brittany, his sumptuous *hôtel particulier* in the Rue de l'Université, and all his eighteenth-century and Art Deco collections. He has also now sold his flat in New York, because he never even spent one night there. Nowadays he limits himself to an apartment near his bookshop in the Rue de Lille, an apartment in Monte Carlo, a house near St Tropez, and a 'typical wooden New England house' in Vermont, which he is 'mad about. Autumn there is as near paradise as one can get to on earth. And it couldn't be more typically American; very rural. I feel that when you're in a certain place, your surroundings should always be typical of that place, and no other. Of course, I almost never have the time to go, but it's nice to know it's there, waiting for me, with its heavenly view of a lake....'

This brings to mind an old saying of Lagerfeld's about couture being 'a floating cloud of a dream, too beautiful to be real'. Perhaps the true function of a fashion designer, then, is to be a dream merchant. Lagerfeld appears to like both the term and the concept. After all, it is in harmony with his view that opera must remain in the sphere of dreams ...and it may point to the subliminal link between the worlds of fashion and opera.

Giulietta

manches
matelassées
soulignées d'une
résille de
perles
comme le
corsage.

bandes de
fourrure
reliées
par des
rangées
de perles

HL
petit talon

RIGHT Didone (sung by
Dunja Vejzovic), wearing
an elaborately decorated
dress, topped with an
imposing crown, in Luca
Ronconi's production of
Les Troyens at La Scala,
Milan, 1982. Berlioz based
his libretto on Virgil's epic
The Aeneid.

❝ You need costumes that make a splash from afar. The stage acts as an amplifier and you have to make bold statements.

ABOVE The Scala chorus in the famous Act IV ballet of *Les Troyens*. This was omitted when the production opened in 1982, but was included in the 1996 revival, for which Lagerfeld designed the additional costumes shown here.

RIGHT Priamo, King of Troy (Luigi Roni), with his queen, Ecuba (Elisabetta Battaglia), dressed in suitably regal attire, in the 1996 revival of *Les Troyens*.

LA RONDINE

ABOVE Soprano Nelly Miricioiu as Magda in Puccini's *La Rondine* ('The Swallow', originally intended as an operetta for Vienna), Monte Carlo Opera, 1992. Her pale pink embroidered bustle dress reflects her 'vie en rose' happiness.

RIGHT Ruggero (Alberto Cupido) with Magda (Nelly Miricioiu) in a striped dress 'shaped like a swallow', mirroring the title of the opera and, like all of Lagerfeld's costumes for this production, helping the singer inhabit her role.

OPPOSITE ABOVE Magda in the elaborate black dress intended to convey the 'matrona'. Nelly Miricioiu's costumes also hid the fact that she was four months pregnant at the time.

OPPOSITE BELOW Sketches for Act II and Act III of *La Rondine*.

> **❝** Just stepping into my costume gave me the character's personality.

NELLY MIRICIOIU, SOPRANO

MANON

RIGHT Manon (Renée Fleming) with Des Grieux (Ramon Vargas) in Jules Massenet's *Manon* at the Metropolitan Opera gala, autumn 1998, at which Fleming sang one act from three different operas and was dressed by three different designers.

KARL LAGERFELD

❝ Opera lives through singers. Without singers it's nothing. But it must remain in the sphere of dreams.

ABOVE AND RIGHT Lagerfeld's design for Manon – a pale-coloured crinoline dress, with flounced lace sleeves and bow trim – was superbly evocative of the eighteenth century. Here Renée Fleming appears in the Gavotte Scene.

OPPOSITE The gala was mounted to celebrate Fleming's artistry and her long association with the Metropolitan Opera. Here she is seen in Lagerfeld's magnificent frilled black cape.

Ottavio and Rosita Missoni

'We Missonis are all about woollens, plaids, stripes and patterns'

When the distinguished director and designer Pier Luigi Pizzi was asked to stage a new production of Donizetti's *Lucia di Lammermoor* for La Scala and the Grand Théâtre de Genève, he decided not to design the costumes himself (something he is both qualified to do and used to doing); nor did he assign the job to an established theatrical costume designer. Instead, he looked to the world of fashion. Along with many male celebrities from the spheres of entertainment and music, including Placido Domingo, Riccardo Muti, Rudolf Nureyev and Roberto Bertolucci, to name but a few, Pizzi was a fan and avid collector of Missoni knitwear. And, as Donizetti's opera is based on Sir Walter Scott's novel *The Bride of Lammermoor* and set in Scotland, who would be more ideal, he thought, than the husband-and-wife team of Ottavio (Tai) and Rosita Missoni, creators of the world's most coveted knitwear?

'I immediately thought of them,' he says, 'because I liked the idea of inventing new, hitherto non-existent Scottish tartans with their help! My departure point for the set was a vast, dark green velvet wall, which would serve like a background in a painting. I wanted all the colour on stage to be provided by the costumes. And who could manage that better than the Missonis?' So Pizzi rang up Tai (who, along with Rosita, had meanwhile become a friend), and, to Tai's amazement, asked if he would be prepared to design the costumes for the forthcoming *Lucia*.

While Rosita was a music lover and had long followed La Scala's productions, Tai 'knew absolutely nothing about *Lucia*, not even what it was, exactly'. But, being by nature a curious and adventurous spirit, he wanted to know all about the story. 'Once I realized that it was set in Scotland, I said OK, no problem,' he recalls. 'Had it been *Otello*, or *Semiramide*, or some opera set in the Caribbean, I would probably have said no.' 'But,' adds Rosita, 'for *Lucia* the answer was yes, because this is our territory. We Missonis are all about woollens, plaids, stripes and patterns, so we would be working on something we knew. Scotland – its history and its costumes – is a panorama we have often visited for our work in fashion. So we knew exactly what to do and how to do it.' Despite this, Rosita admits that, left to her own devices, she would have refused the job because the Scala production, scheduled for March 1983, clashed with the presentation of the Missoni autumn/winter 1984 collection.

Tai, however, was undaunted, even though he had never designed for the theatre before, because the design involved knits, prints, waistcoats and other familiar Missoni features. 'Knowing exactly what kind of textures, stitches and materials were needed, I decided to place the responsibility for the whole thing, down to the last tam o'shanter, on my shoulders. Of course, this involved a vertiginous amount of work. The costumes were made one by one; there were two or three different kinds of beret to suit different facial types and shapes; plus jewelry, which also had to be designed and made.'

OPPOSITE Sketch of a man's costume for Donizetti's *Lucia di Lammermoor* at La Scala, Milan, 1983. The director, Pier Luigi Pizzi, liked the idea of inventing new Scottish tartans.

As soon as the Missonis had accepted the commission, work started on designing the fabrics. 'We produced some stitches which, I think, were quite beautiful,' says Rosita. To begin with, Tai designed a series of special fabrics that were ideal for waistcoats and jackets. He proudly remembers actually making most of the costumes before he drew a single sketch — a feat of which he had always professed himself incapable, and one which greatly amused his wife at the time. She had been married to Tai for many years and had always taken him at his word when he maintained that he could not cut fabric. 'But one day I walked into his studio and there he was, in the midst of his excitement in the creative process, actually cutting a shepherd's cape himself. Without admitting or even realizing it, he was able to cut fabrics and clothes perfectly to obtain the desired effect!'

Tai's biggest challenge was dressing the chorus, especially since so many of the costumes would be viewed at the same time. 'I had no experience of putting a hundred and forty people on stage simultaneously, coordinating and arranging the costumes so that the colours and shapes would harmonize and present a well-thought-out, integrated, visual image. But everything worked out well. As I didn't know exactly how the chorus would be placed or moved around, I decided I could play with groups of colours. So I focused on the Scots of that century, including groups of shepherds with tartan capes, not a bit like the red/green/black tartan costumes one sees today even on biscuit boxes, or anything "courtly", but on an overall pastoral feel in Scottish hues — lilac-y, heather-y shades, mixed with terracotta.'

The costumes for the principal characters were more luxurious. While Tai designed all the men's costumes, Rosita was responsible for dressing the heroine, Lucia — a great 'diva role', and one most famously taken by Maria Callas and Joan Sutherland. For this production, Luciana Serra was to make her eagerly awaited debut at La Scala. Rosita was fully conscious of how important it was for her costumes to be extra-special. 'In her case,' explains Rosita, 'they *were* courtly. And as Luciana Serra is a good-looking woman, she carried them off beautifully.' There were three costumes in all: a long blue dress; a long white dress for the Mad Scene; and a long tunic in a pleated knit that the Missonis were already showing in their collection. 'I remember that one day Pier Luigi Pizzi came to our studio and, while we were discussing the costumes, I suddenly saw this particular roll of fabric tucked away in a corner. So I unrolled it and saw that he was immediately fascinated by its possibilities.'

While Rosita busied herself with Serra's dresses, Tai, who had started listening to the music, was preparing Luciano Pavarotti's 'cavaliere nero' costume: a jacket 'also very similar to one I was showing in our collection'. As Tai recalls, Pavarotti loved his costume so much that he asked to keep it (in fact, Pavarotti — who,

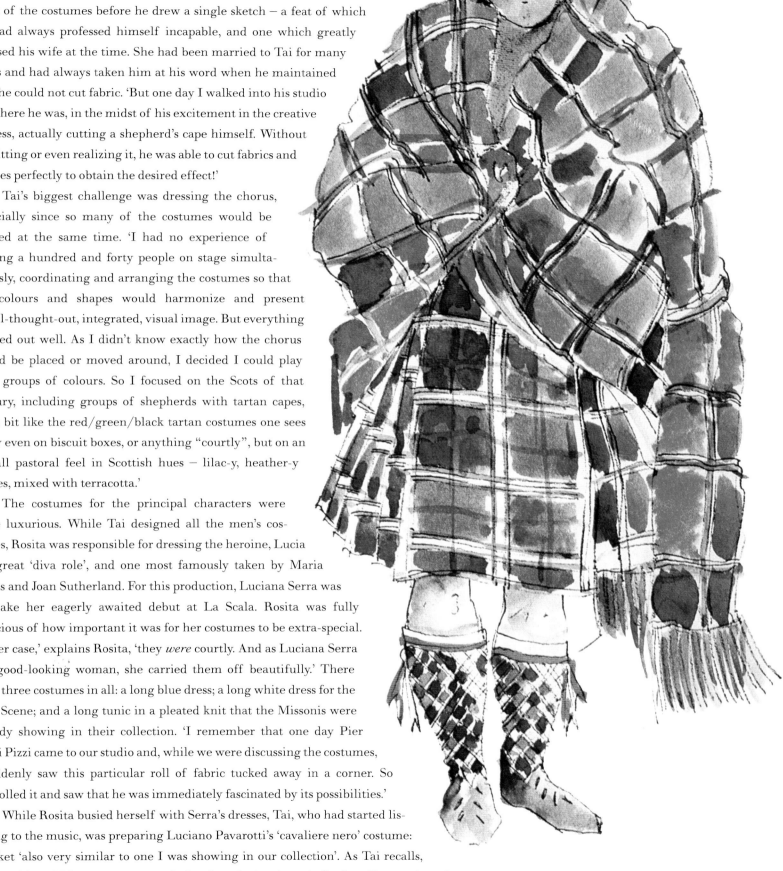

BELOW Sketch of a costume for *Lucia di Lammermoor*. Ottavio Missoni knew nothing about the opera, but felt comfortable with *Lucia* once he realized that it was set in familiar territory – Scotland.

despite his size, was always a snazzy dresser – kept *all* his costumes at the end of the run). The other principals were equally delighted. Pizzi notes that 'everyone who sang in this production and wore the Missoni costumes had a tendency to want to take them home…. It became imperative to lock them up after every performance!' Luciana Serra was so happy to discover Missoni clothes that she continued to wear them in real life. The only people who were less happy were the members of the chorus because they felt too hot moving about the stage in costumes that were mostly woollen – kilts, vests, capes, shawls, socks and caps – instead of the usual synthetic, theatrical fabrics to which they were accustomed.

In contrast to usual practice, all the costumes were produced at the Missoni workshops in Sumirago, about an hour's drive from Milan, rather than at La Scala itself. This provoked a strike of the theatre's entire wardrobe department, who wanted the costumes made on site. 'But it wouldn't have been possible without our specialist machines,' explains Tai. 'We even offered to make them a present of the costumes, but they still refused. So the Scala workshops had to be paid by the theatre for doing nothing, and we had to deduct the sum from our own fee.'

The fittings took place in the singers' dressing rooms, and 'the biggest emotion', according to Rosita, was wrapping and pinning the cape on Pavarotti. 'Fitting such a megastar in his dressing room was a huge thrill for me. And I also remember that my daughter Angela [now head of Women's Design in the firm] had just had a baby and was breastfeeding throughout the fittings in Pavarotti's and Luciana Serra's dressing rooms!' Unfortunately, Pavarotti, who was returning to La Scala after a few years' absence, was having difficulty at the time with some of the vocal challenges of the role. As Pizzi recalls, 'Although he loved his costume, he had other, more important issues to cope with.'

This staging of *Lucia* was the first time that Pizzi had collaborated with fashion designers in a full production (he had once staged a spectacle entitled 'A Tribute to Maria Callas' at the Verona Arena, for which Roberto Capucci, Karl Lagerfeld for Fendi, Trussardi, Donatella Girombelli and Gianfranco Ferré had contributed a costume each). Pizzi usually designs the costumes for his own productions, and has them made under his supervision, either in-house at the various theatres or at famous theatrical ateliers such as Tirelli in Rome. He was pleasantly surprised to discover that, although this was the Missonis' first foray into operatic design, he didn't need to 'teach' them anything, 'only to voice specific requests'. 'And in allowing them complete freedom, we nevertheless worked in unison. Far from producing a mere spectacle, they considered every aspect and every character of the opera. Their approach was anything but superficial. There was a precise reason behind every decision and every choice.'

Pizzi professed himself totally satisfied with the result. Indeed, although his production, with its very dark, very northern sets, was criticized in the press, the Missonis' costumes were highly praised. When asked if he would have liked to collaborate on an opera with any other fashion designers, he replied, 'Yes, with Giorgio Armani, the late Gianni Versace and the late Yves Saint Laurent.' The experience also proved fascinating and educational for both Missonis because 'of course, designing for the theatre is a completely different discipline from producing a fashion collection. In the theatre you have a story that you have to adhere to and try to interpret visually, whereas in fashion you are free – or at least, you *think* you are free because, fashion being fashion, it gives you the possibility to change things up to the very last moment before a collection goes on the runway.'

Tai notes, however, that opera also has its own risky spontaneity. 'At the finale, after the Mad Scene, when the tenor sings the beautiful aria "*Tu che a Dio spiegasti l'ali, o bell'alma innamorata*", Pavarotti muffled a note and a loud boo was heard. So Pizzi, who had rehearsed the curtain calls meticulously, changed course at the last minute and had everyone come forward and bow together, hand in hand, so that no single singer could get booed. Someone,' Tai recalls with a chuckle, 'said he should have rehearsed for boos and not for ovations!'

ABOVE Ottavio Missoni, the director Pier Luigi Pizzi and Rosita Missoni, all wearing Missoni knits, during discussions for their production of *Lucia di Lammermoor*, which coincided with the presentation of the Missoni autumn/winter 1984 collection at Milan Fashion Week.

❝ In the theatre you have a story that you have to adhere to and try to interpret visually, whereas in fashion you are free – or at least, you *think* you are free.

Would the Missonis like to design for the opera again? 'No, I don't think so,' says Tai. 'It's too great a risk for very little reward! *Lucia* was a huge undertaking and involved a colossal amount of work, especially the way we did it – not only designing both fabrics and costumes but also manufacturing all those hundred and forty-plus costumes ourselves. But it was worth it. We really enjoyed it and felt very pleased with ourselves at the end.' Rosita agrees, but, fresh from the triumphant reception of her designs for the Hotel Missoni in Edinburgh (Scotland again), she beams, 'I never want to do another opera. I want to do more hotels!'

OVERLEAF Edgardo (Luciano Pavarotti) and Lucia (Luciana Serra), surrounded by the chorus in *Lucia di Lammermoor* at La Scala, Milan, 1983. Ottavio Missoni designed a different costume for each member of the chorus.

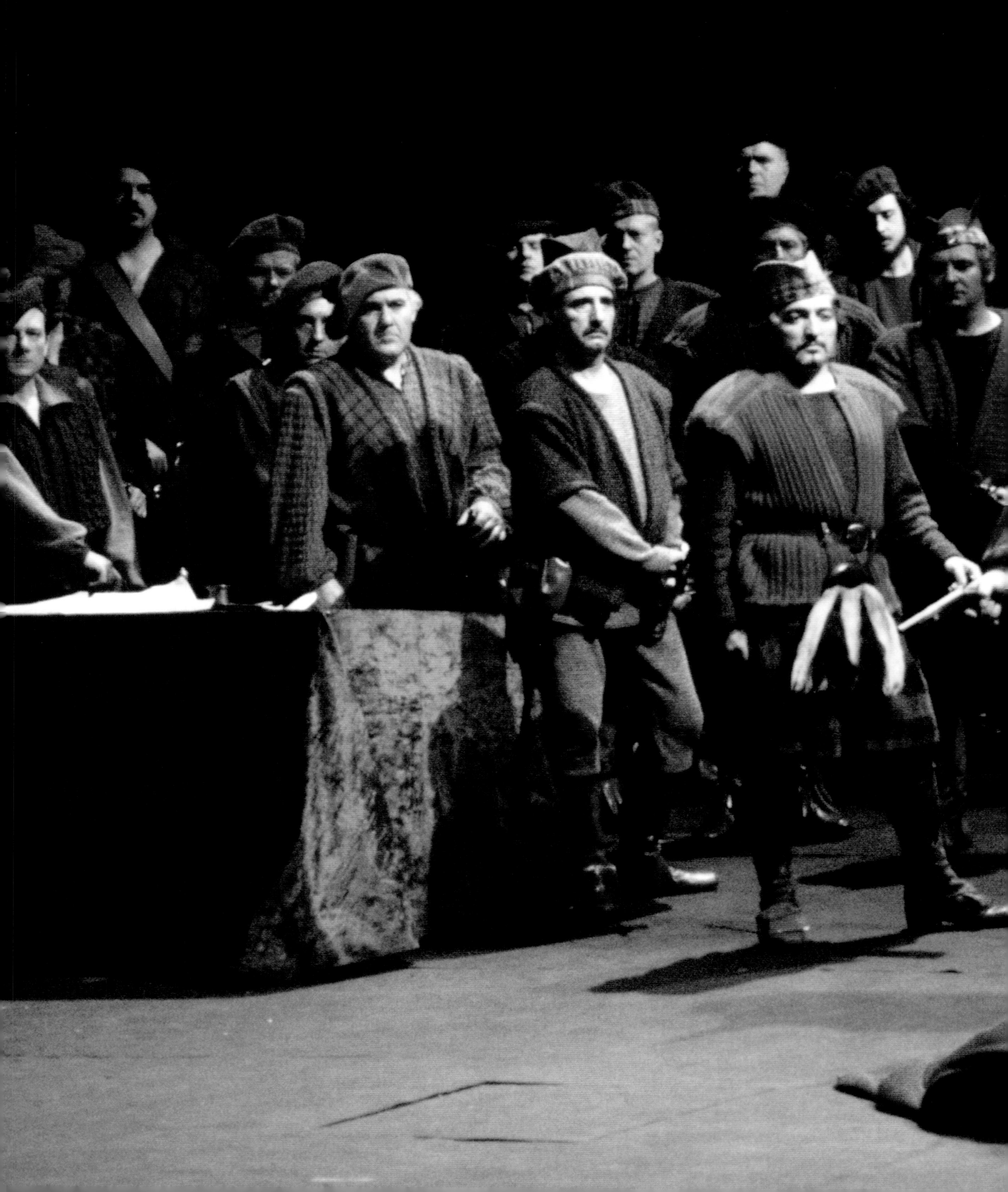

RIGHT AND OPPOSITE
Sketches of men's
costumes for *Lucia di
Lammermoor*, showing
traditional elements,
including medieval-
style caps, large capes,
doublets, kilt, tartan
hose and gartered socks.

90

OPPOSITE LEFT AND RIGHT
Sketches of costumes for
Lucia. Most of the men's
costumes were rustic,
based on simple medieval
Scottish shepherds' clothes,
but Lucia's wardrobe was
distinctly courtly.

RIGHT Lucia (Luciana Serra)
in a floor-length, royal blue
dress, with a distinctive ruff
at the neck.

** "** We produced some stitches which, I think, were quite beautiful, and which would have been impossible without our specialist machines.

This uncharacteristically plain white dress was designed by Rosita Missoni for the famous Mad Scene, in which Lucia (sung by Luciana Serra) raves in a vocal tour de force. Having been forced to betray the man she loves and marry another, Lucia stabs her new husband to death on their wedding night.

LEFT AND OPPOSITE ABOVE
Sketches of costumes for *Lucia di Lammermoor*, showing traditional period details, including tam o'shanters and feathered caps, fringed capes, tartan sashes with brooches and kilts with sporrans.

OPPOSITE BELOW Ottavio Missoni designed special fabrics in shades of lilac and heather with terracotta. He also created several kinds of headgear and belts.

Miuccia
Prada

'My favourite thing was experimenting in a different field, and such a difficult one'

If there is anything in the operatic world that is tantamount to 'jumping in at the deep end', it is singing, conducting, designing sets or designing costumes for a production at the Metropolitan Opera in New York – especially when you are a first-time singer, conductor or designer. Yet that is just what the fearless individualist Miuccia Prada did, and pulled off with remarkable success, when she created the costumes for the first airing at the Met of Verdi's early masterpiece, *Attila*.

The conductor was Riccardo Muti, a renowned Verdi champion, and the director was Pierre Audi, founder of the Almeida Theatre and Artistic Director of the Netherlands Opera and Holland Festival, both making their Met debuts. The set designers were Jacques Herzog and Pierre de Meuron – winners of the Pritzker Prize, the highest accolade in architecture, and the team responsible for such iconic buildings as Tate Modern in London and the Beijing 'Bird's Nest' National Stadium. Having previously designed sets for Wagner's *Tristan und Isolde* at the Berlin State Opera, the duo noted, 'We never solved all the technical problems in Berlin, but nevertheless it was a very interesting first experience. That is why we accepted a second one.'

The Herzog & de Meuron commission was the brainwave of the Met's General Manager, Peter Gelb. As was the case with Christian Lacroix (see p. 44), Gelb wanted to bring the best and most creative designers to work at the Met. Pierre Audi recalls: 'Peter Gelb wanted me to do this production with an artist of his choice. Given my long experience in collaborating with artists – [Georg] Baselitz, Yannis Kounelis, [Karel] Appel, Anish Kapoor, etc. – he suggested the architectural duo of Herzog & de Meuron, to which I agreed immediately. He approached them himself. Having agreed, Jacques Herzog wanted Miuccia Prada to design the costumes and he did everything he could to persuade her to join the team, after much initial hesitation on her part.' This was hardly surprising, given the fact that, apart from anything else, the rehearsals and premiere were scheduled for the very month that she had to present her autumn/winter 2010 collections in Milan.

In the end, however, the intrepid Ms Prada consented. 'Jacques Herzog and Pierre de Meuron simply asked me to be part of the project. I like working with them. Since I also like opera, *Attila* and Maestro Muti, I said yes.' The architects put forward this highly erudite woman, with broad interests, eclectic tastes and the adventurous spirit that had prompted her to spend five years studying and performing mime at Milan's famous Teatro Piccolo, because 'we have known each other for many years and worked on many architectural projects, where she always involved herself very strongly. It was clear that Miuccia would be a great partner in many things other than just talking about fashion or architecture. After Peter Gelb and Pierre Audi invited us to design the sets, asking Miuccia was an almost immediate, spontaneous reaction. Of course, we asked both of them if they liked the idea…and, of course, they did.'

OPPOSITE Sketch of the Pope for Verdi's *Attila* at the Metropolitan Opera, New York, 2010. The part of the Pope was sung, in a cameo performance, by the bass Samuel Ramey, himself a famous erstwhile interpreter of the role of Attila.

The selection of costume designer by set designer is unusual in the world of opera. As Gelb explains, 'It is really up to the director to decide who the members of his or her creative team will be, and I generally agree with their choices, although I sometimes make suggestions. For example, Anthony Minghella chose Han Feng to design the brilliant costumes for *Madama Butterfly*. *Attila* was a little different, since it was Herzog & de Meuron who suggested Miuccia Prada, as they had an ongoing collaboration with her, and the director, Pierre Audi, agreed. She certainly studied the opera closely and worked in tandem with the director and the scenic designers. Collaborations only work when everyone is in agreement.'

Audi, whose avowed aim is 'to provide innovative music and theatre productions of high quality, in which each theatrical discipline takes an equal part', particularly enjoys working with artists who are not professional designers (Yannis Kounelis, for example, collaborated on Morton Feldman's one-act opera *Neither* in Amsterdam, and Anish Kapoor on Debussy's *Pelléas et Mélisande* at the Théâtre Royal de la Monnaie in Brussels). Audi is notably tolerant of his collaborators' idiosyncrasies. 'Working with artists has always been interesting for me. My approach when working with them is to enjoy their instinctive reaction to the material — music and libretto — and to try to make their contribution work in the action and the totality. So I make the costumes interact and function in the abstraction by not making the production too busy, but also not too simple.'

Indeed, Audi's productions are often minimalist. As he explained in a newspaper interview: 'I'm a storyteller…and, paradoxically, what is nice for a storyteller is to work with an artist who is not necessarily a storyteller but a symbolist. These are not compatible approaches, but two points of view living together can make a production very interesting…. An artist can only come up with one idea for an opera or play. With a [professional] set or costume designer you can say, "Offer me five options; a menu." But every artist I've worked with is incapable of doing that. So, as a director you have to look at the result and then figure out: "How do I tell the story? How do I make this work?" What is fabulous about working with artists is that this degree of concentration offers the possibility of a new meaning. If all you want is options, you should hire a stage designer!'

Attila is not an easy work to mount. Set in the fifth century, it depicts the collapse of the remnants of the western Roman Empire following a wave of attacks from 'barbarians', in this case Attila the Hun, who sacked numerous Italian cities but was stopped outside Rome by Pope Leo VI (this historical encounter is turned by Verdi into one of the opera's most compelling scenes). Attila falls in love with the defeated warrior princess, Odabella, whose father he has killed. She and other Italian patriots, including her fiancé Foresto and a double-dealing general, Ezio, are determined to bring about Attila's destruction. Eventually Odabella stabs him to death during their wedding feast.

The opera was premiered in Venice in 1846 — a time when the movement for the unification of Italy and its liberation from the foreigners who still ruled large parts of it, including Venice, was at its peak.

Verdi was an ardent and committed champion. According to Pierre Audi, in *Attila* 'Verdi gives us a message that is very contemporary: political dominance in the end is a completely negative development. Personal freedom and emotional fulfilment are far more important. It's a story about what appears to be a hero but is, in fact, an anti-hero.'

Jacques Herzog and Pierre de Meuron found that 'designing this opera was tough work, because it cannot be so easily grasped. It does not open itself so easily to contemporary understanding.... The historical narration of the birth of a nation dominates the relatively simple psychological structure of the protagonists. Because this is so, the collaboration had to be very intense, very in-depth. We had lengthy discussions.... Politics, history and many other fields were involved to prepare the terrain, so to speak, before we could do the job properly.'

The set designs were extremely atmospheric and evocative of the period, yet resonant with modern references to destruction and displaced peoples. The creators recall: 'We liked the fact that *Attila* is based on Verdi's description of a destroyed city and various scenes in forests between Venice and Rome. Staying quite close to his descriptions gave us

> ❝ I wanted to work as a fashion designer rather than a costume designer…approaching themes that I had already approached and making them relevant to this opera.

the opportunity to develop two strong images for the whole opera: the rubble and the forest.' As noted in the playbill published for the Met premiere: '*Attila* describes the moment in history when an old world, an antique world, is collapsing and something new is rising out of the rubble. It's a moment of uncertainty and instability, and new powers are emerging. It's not unlike a situation we live in right now.'

Audi agrees, and adds that the stage design, and the team's decision to concentrate on the tragedy of the characters, helped to make this clear. 'Miuccia Prada's contribution towards this end was a very important artistic factor. Her work is usually very pure and very simple, and I think that her designs for *Attila* were very musical and brought out the characters, not so much in an operatic as in a natural way. They made the emotional aspect of the opera more vibrant.'

Prada herself explains that she tried 'to express my vision of the characters from a psychological and historical point of view, and what the characters mean to me today. You have to do it in a way that is contemporary and understandable. I wanted to work as a fashion designer rather than a costume designer…also approaching themes that I had already approached and making them relevant to this opera.'

Prada's striking costumes did just that. In the opening scene, Attila's nappa leather overcoat was a modern take on the cape. Together with his glowing helmet, it represented the character's strength. The helmet, a modern interpretation of the concept of the crown, was inspired by urban living but given both an antiquated effect and LED lights — a recurring motif in the costumes of many of the characters. Audi liked 'the simplicity of the shapes Miuccia proposed, and the materials. Attila had two "looks", which made the face of the singer stand out, and this helped us a lot. The relatively sober nature of this

OPPOSITE Sketch for one of the Italian general Ezio's guards. The guards' uniforms were made contemporary by the use of Prada T-shirts and plastic camouflage-patterned shields given a modern shape.

costume corresponded to the troubled and tormented nature of a conqueror with a deep melancholy and loneliness.' During the Wedding Scene, Attila wore his overcoat draped over one shoulder, to enhance the idea of an ancient mantle, over a T-shirt of gold silk satin detailed with metal, denoting opulence and luxury.

The overcoat worn by Attila's confidant, Uldino, was created out of a special fabric of woven jacquard with a leopard-print effect reminiscent of Prada's 2006 women's collection. The *animalier* effect conveyed by the graphic element in the fabric, plus the cloak draped on Uldino's back like a primitive animal skin, were designed to emphasize the character's affiliation to the barbarian cohort. The 'eco-beaver' fur chosen to detail the costume of Attila's guards was also intended to underline the characters' barbaric origins, while creating the effect of protective armour over the chest and legs. The frontal panels were completed by a nylon ribbon with a metal buckle – a symbol of the Prada brand and similar to the closure of Attila's overcoat. As Prada herself reported in a newspaper interview: 'My challenge was to find a balance between classicism and Prada; to do something meaningful and contemporary, but with a sense of timelessness; to find fabrics and decorations that I like now, but that could express feelings beyond time.'

The barbarians' costumes contrasted sharply with the elegant clothes worn by the Romans, led by General Ezio. He sported a cloak that evoked the ancient world but was modernized by saffiano leather shoulder pads, featuring lights. His shirt was made of radzmire, a classic Prada fabric, decorated with studs – a reference to both the Roman world and the Prada autumn/winter 2009 menswear collection. 'Ezio's costume was a military uniform, showing off the vain pride of the last Roman general,' says Audi. 'Originally Miuccia wanted to show him as a fake, a two-faced man, which he is in the story of this opera, but Maestro Muti insisted that he should be heroic and noble.' The general's guards wore blue trousers and black boots with Prada T-shirts – symbols of everyday life – and shields that were made out of a plastic material covered with a camouflage pattern.

One of the most elegant costumes was the doublebreasted overcoat worn by the knight Foresto, Odabella's fiancé, made of cashgora double antic, a cashmere and angora fabric, trimmed in metal for a naturally crumpled look. The aim was for the overcoat to dominate this figure, whose valiant, combative personality was also reflected in Prada's choice of straps – a mix of saffiano and neoprene, joined by a belt with metal-work reminiscent of the clasp on Ezio's cape and symbolic of the two characters' Italian origins. Under his cape, Foresto wore a shirt of stretch poplin – another classic Prada fabric – with a stud-decorated collar inspired by Prada's autumn/winter 2009 menswear collection. According to Audi, 'Foresto was intended by Miuccia in her first designs as a rather abstract, tightly dressed, civilian figure. But in the end, Ezio and Foresto ended up looking more "operatic" than Miuccia intended.'

The ecclesiastical symbolism of the pope, 'Papa Leone', was expressed by the use of a mitre and red silk duchesse slippers. The basic outfit was a long T-shirt made of raso doppio tec, an elegant, hi-tech Prada fabric. The pope's pastoral staff was a simple, unadorned cross in white wood, while his smoky resin crucifix was decorated with metal elements and studs, instead of gems, thus offering a reinterpretation of the clergy's precious accessories and investing them with an industrial quality for a 'distressed' look, which, throughout, expresses the act of fighting.

Odabella, the formidable Aquileian warrior princess, also sported an impressive overcoat – the symbol of strength that appeared in so many of the main characters' costumes. Hers was made of leather, lined with metal for the crumpled look (again expressive of battle), and decorated at the back with large numbers of embroidered sequins in coordinating colours. Her diadem was a modern metal band with LED lights. 'Odabella is proud and strong; an amazon with a heart but also a determination for revenge – a Greek tragedienne,' notes Audi. 'The costume here had an almost masculine force, without taking any of the feminine appeal of the figure away.' In the Wedding Banquet Scene, Odabella's outfit took the form of a dramatic floor-length T-shirt in embellished gold silk.

One of the biggest challenges in designing costumes for operas such as *Attila*, which feature large crowd scenes made up of many different characters – in this case, slaves, dancers, hermits, defeated Aquileians, and so on – is dressing the chorus, or rather the several choruses. Peter Gelb acknowledges how complicated Miuccia Prada's task was, 'since there were so many costumes to design and build'. She conceived the main chorus as being dressed in a minimal and repetitive fashion, in tones of grey and military green used for both their Prada-style T-shirts and their wide-cut trousers, trimmed with metal for a vintage look. The chorus appeared in the darkness, wearing luminous head coverings. Audi remembers them 'in their simplicity as the most beautiful and original costumes I've ever seen used on a chorus. Originally they were intended to be hidden in the set. But during the last rehearsals, the conductor demanded that they be removed from the set and placed in front. These costumes survived this change very well. They worked beautifully and remain totally memorable.'

But there is more than one kind of crowd in this opera. Despite Ms Prada's alleged protestation that she 'could not dress these people, I can dress only models', each grouping was given costumes that were highly original, imaginative and evocative of time and place, but at the same time 'modern'. The chorus of slaves was given outfits with primitive silhouettes, in devoré silk, frayed and distressed by hand to achieve a 'worn' effect. The outfits had three different necklines (V, round and boat), frayed calfskin belts and fan pleating – all echoes of the world of Prada. The chorus of dancers was given a look inspired by the traffic of contemporary metropolises. The dancers wore T-shirts, again with three different necklines, 'soiled' with transparent silicone for a textural and translucent effect, and worn with belts printed to look like truck tyres, decorated with black rubber chains. The chorus of Aquileians, meanwhile, was dressed in primitive fashion with artificial fur in brown shades, evocative of ancient sacrifices, paired with simple belts and worn with grey jersey trousers. Within this group, and among the furs,

ABOVE Sketch for Odabella's wedding dress, a floor-length T-shirt in gold silk, trimmed in metal and enriched with gold embroidered sequins and feathers.

were some Prada T-shirts torn and 'soiled' with tar and tempera to create the image of a conquered people.

The sheer number of cast members involved in all these scenes indicates the magnitude of the task facing the costume designer. In addition, as Audi points out: 'In rehearsals, a production develops in a way that sometimes affects how appropriate the costumes are to movements on the set. Furthermore, in a big theatre – and the Met has nearly four thousand seats – costumes look very different from a huge distance, and materials can either work better than expected or worse. And then adaptations and adjustments are needed. Miuccia was amazing to work with. She wanted to fight for a "concept" and was anxious to do well. She was so committed, intense, concerned for the totality, and at the same time not devoid of a sense of humour, something you often need in the operatic profession!'

The production received a mixed reception on the opening night. While Riccardo Muti and the singers received vociferous applause, the production was booed by a certain section of the Met audience, who, until the advent of Peter Gelb, were largely unused to unconventional stagings (and this opera is rarely mounted). There is no doubt, however, that an altogether memorable evening was created.

Herzog & de Meuron and Miuccia Prada remain open to the possibility of further forays into opera. 'My favourite thing about this project was experimenting in a different field, and such a difficult one,' says Prada. 'With costumes, the starting point is quite different because the story is already there and there are some real restrictions imposed by the set and the opera itself.' She says she would enjoy designing costumes for *Tosca*, one of her favourite operas.

Herzog & de Meuron also feel that 'with the experience we have collected, it will be interesting to explore the field of opera, and even ballet, further.... It depends on what that opera would be, and who else would be involved.... We would certainly want to continue to work with Miuccia. She is not someone who repeats her style, but who works conceptually. In this we have a similar approach in tackling new things. It would be interesting to complete the team with a director who comes from film rather than the theatre …and for sure the conductor should have a sense for things other than "only" music. In such a collaboration, the idea that one can learn from another is very important.'

Pierre Audi would also 'love to work with Miuccia again; she is a true genius'. But he emphasizes that the production should be based on teamwork from an early stage, before a concept is decided upon. 'Ideally,' he says, 'there should be enough time in Miuccia's schedule for her to watch the production developing and building itself up during stage rehearsals and coming to life musically – a magical process – because her work is musical and innovative in its simplicity and power. It combines the right degree of poetry and meaning, which opera needs to thrive on if it is to survive the twenty-first century.'

ABOVE Sketch for a citizen of Aquileia, dressed in primitive fashion, with belted artificial fur over T-shirts and simple grey jersey trousers.

PREVIOUS PAGES The Rubble, one of the two powerful sets devised by the award-winning Swiss architects Herzog & de Meuron for the Metropolitan Opera production of *Attila*, 2010. It brilliantly evokes the ravages of wars past and present. The male chorus sits underneath, dressed in a minimal fashion in tones of grey and military green.

ABOVE Attila (Ildar Abdrazakov) with his faithful confidant Uldino (Russell Thomas) in the Forest, the second of Herzog & de Meuron's extraordinary sets. Uldino's draped cloak and leopard-print overcoat signal his affiliation to the barbarian horde.

LEFT AND OPPOSITE ABOVE The Roman general Ezio (sung by Giovanni Meoni), wearing a cloak designed to evoke the ancient world but with the modernizing touch of saffiano leather shoulder pads featuring LED lights.

OPPOSITE BELOW Attila (Ildar Abdrazakov), as he appears in the opening scene, carrying a gleaming, feathered helmet and sporting a nappa leather overcoat, leather shirt and rumpled black flannel trousers that represent his virile strength.

66 Ezio's costume was
a military uniform,
showing off the vain pride
of the last Roman general.

PIERRE AUDI, DIRECTOR

𝅮 Odabella is proud and strong; an amazon with a heart but also a determination for revenge – a Greek tragedienne.

PIERRE AUDI, DIRECTOR

RIGHT Sketch of a costume for Odabella, including a studded headpiece and a floor-length coat in brown leather, trimmed with feathers.

BELOW Odabella (sung by mezzo-turned-soprano Violeta Urmana) with her maids, preparing for her encounter with Attila. Her costume exudes an almost masculine strength without taking away any of her feminine appeal.

OPPOSITE Odabella (Violeta Urmana) with Attila (Ildar Abdrazakov), the Hun invader who has killed her father but is fatally captivated by her charms. The pair's nappa leather overcoats are detailed in metal to create a crumpled effect.

'What prompted me to accept was the fact that opera is so over the top, so exotic!'

Zandra Rhodes has always been the most 'theatrical' of fashion designers. Bursting onto the London scene in around 1970, she took it by storm and set the tone for what was to follow for more than a decade, turning fashion into costume and transforming her environment into pure theatre. Her phantasmagoric, totally original clothes were snapped up by Fortnum & Mason, then London's most exclusive store, where the directors devoted the shop's entire window display to her. This led not only to a four-page spread in British *Vogue*, but also to her debut as a costume designer for the theatre. The distinguished actress Irene Worth happened to see Fortnum's windows and was so overwhelmed that she decided this was what she wanted to wear in a forthcoming production of Edward Albee's play, *Tiny Alice*. So she brought the play's director to Fortnum's and together they bought the voluminous, full-length, printed yellow felt opera coat and the sea-green, printed chiffon kaftan – both of which Worth eventually donated to the Victoria and Albert Museum.

Rhodes soon became as famous for her own unique appearance as for her psychedelic creations. Long before the punk movement was even heard of, she was painting her cheeks and hair royal blue or emerald green, before finally settling on her trademark fuchsia. In the mid-1970s, when the punk look eventually took hold, she brought it into the drawing room with her silk jersey tops complete with strategically placed slits and safety pins (this was nearly two decades before Gianni Versace's 'safety-pin' dress famously sported by Elizabeth Hurley and revised by Christopher Kane for the younger Versace range, Versus, in 2010). Yet, amazingly, for such an obviously theatrical designer, it was not until 2001 that Rhodes was asked to design costumes for the opera.

By the time the invitation came, Rhodes had opened her visually arresting Fashion and Textile Museum in Bermondsey, near London Bridge – a vibrant orange and fuschia building designed by the celebrated architect Ricardo Legorreta. The building also contains Rhodes's workshop – where she designs and prints her fabrics, as well as makes the clothing for her collections – and her amazing, colourful home, which could easily double as an operatic set.

As it turned out, it was Rhodes's home-from-home in San Diego, California, that provided the impetus for the invitation to the stage. Ian Campbell, the adventurous General Director of San Diego Opera, was well acquainted with Rhodes's fashion designs and her particular love of colour and way with fabric. When he arrived at San Diego and discovered that she lived in the city for part of the year, the seed for a possible collaboration was sown. 'But it really germinated,' he notes, 'when I first visited her home for dinner and was absolutely bowled over. The fabrics, colours and taste throughout the house simply made my mind start playing with ideas for operatic designs. By the end of dinner, I knew I had to find a way to work with her.'

When, soon afterwards, Campbell suggested that Rhodes design the costumes for a forthcoming production of *The Magic Flute*, her reaction was modest. She pointed out that she had no experience of operatic design and didn't even know much about opera. However, she quickly warmed to the opportunity of having a bigger 'runway', a larger canvas on which to work, than that provided by fashion. 'What prompted me to accept,' she says, 'was the fact that opera is so over the top, so exotic! Until I came to live in San Diego I had hardly ever visited an opera house. But after accepting the assignment, it became quite an obsession, and now I love it and listen to it all the time, especially when trying to think my way into specific scenes and how they should look.'

Of the process of designing for the opera (while creating actual designs, she says she tends to listen to the BBC's Radio 4, because she likes 'things going into my brain as I work'), she notes: 'I suppose I felt that the experience was really like doing a very, very exotic dress show, where the clothes are not there *per se*, but in order to say something specific about the various characters.' In common with most couturiers who have designed for the opera, Rhodes notes that this is the fundamental difference between fashion and costume design. Naturally, it is also a totally different discipline from the technical point of view. 'In real-life clothes, you have to focus on detail, whereas on stage you have to make broad-brush statements because you're not going to be seeing those costumes at close quarters. So you've got to think, "Is this or that costume going to be impressive enough from a distance?" Costumes also have to be quite practical, which places some restrictions on the sorts of materials you can use as a stage costumier. The singers have to be able to move around without being too hot, because the act of singing produces terrific body heat. Funnily enough, that's something costume designers don't always take into account.' (Tai and Rosita Missoni confess to having made that very mistake with their heavy knits for the chorus in *Lucia di Lammermoor* at La Scala; see p. 86.)

As soon as Rhodes accepted Campbell's offer, she committed herself to learning more about *The Magic Flute*. According to Campbell, she made absolutely no conditions 'other than for us to recognize that, as her experience of stage design was minimal, we would need to teach her a few "tricks". The director, Michael Hampe, would explain the meaning of certain scenes and what each of the characters stood for, and then she would think about it and come up with an appropriate costume: for example, Sarastro, the High Priest, stands for the sun, symbolizing light, while the Queen of the Night stands for the opposite....'

For this production Hampe had already decided that the Queen of the Night should descend to the stage, riding on the moon. 'So,' recalls Rhodes, 'I said that if her cloak was meant to be the night sky, then let's make it *look* like the night sky. I suggested that it seemed logical to give her a cloak that unfolds as night descends onto the stage and that the way to achieve this effect was by lowering a curtain made to look like a cloak. It was very cleverly done. In fact, we had to have two cloaks, two separate pieces of scenery: one that came up to the bottom of the cradle onto which she was strapped – a platform shaped like the moon, which was lowered from a height of about 40 feet – and another behind her

ABOVE Sketch for Papagena in Mozart's *The Magic Flute* at the San Diego Opera, 2001. This marked Zandra Rhodes's first foray into opera, and imbued her with a lasting passion for the genre.

that unfolded gradually, timed so that her cloak appeared to cover the entire stage, which turned into the night sky as she descended in her moon-shaped cradle. This was pure invention – unlike the yellow robes worn by the priests, which were a man's version of a jacket in my fashion collection!'

All the priests were bald (except for the two guarding Sarastro's temple and singing '*Zurück*' ['Go back'] at the hero Tamino's arrival). Sarastro himself was given yellow hair that stood up on end, and a yellow iridescent pleated cape that opened like a peacock's tail. The face and hands of Sarastro's slave Monostatos and all the other slaves were painted blue, and they had manacles and tattoos stuck onto their pink body stockings, which were then painted another shade of blue so that the bodies looked muscular.

One of the finest touches was the use of iridescent fabric, which seemed to turn to ultraviolet whenever Tamino's magic flute or his companion Papageno's magic bells (represented by a glockenspiel) were played, or whenever the lighting was changed, or when the troupe of magically tamed beasts was brought in – as Rhodes recalls, 'among them a crocodile, a hippopotamus covered in mirrors and pearls, pink fluorescent monkeys that glowed in the dark, two griffins and eight-foot-tall lions with open jaws and Trojan shields; the dragons alone had forty people under them!'

With the exception of the spectacular stuffed animals, which were fabricated in London, all the costumes were made in San Diego. The budget was $250,000 for the sets and $200,000 for the costumes. Rhodes particularly enjoyed designing for the chorus, 'who were all sizes'. She wanted the characters to belong to no country in particular, so she dressed them 'to look vaguely golden, with some bits of my prints, plus fabrics from the nearby small towns on the Mexican border and some from a pile of old ethnic cushions that were applied onto a wrap…all sorts of mad things such as these, for which I have to thank Missy West, who worked for Santa Fe Opera and spent six months of the year in San Diego and proved amazing, as did the guy who provided all the armour'.

From the moment Rhodes's involvement in the production was announced, there was immense interest and excitement. Some of the designs were previewed at the Museum of Contemporary Art in nearby La Jolla, and Ian Campbell still remembers the extraordinary 'buzz' before the opening. Once the production was finally staged, the costumes were praised in the press and adored by the public, and 'such was the affection of the first-night audience for Rhodes – a well-established figure in San Diego – that all three thousand opera-goers wore boas made of pink feathers in recognition of her signature colour – and hair'. The production in due course received accolades, including being awarded the Best Live Theatrical Styling Prize in the annual Hollywood Make-Up Artist and Hair Stylist Guild Awards in February 2002.

On the strength of her success, Rhodes was invited to design both costumes and sets for the San Diego Opera production of Bizet's *The Pearl Fishers* in 2004. Designing both aspects was an altogether new departure, and Rhodes felt enormously excited and challenged by the project. The director of the production was Andrew Sinclair, Staff Director at the Royal Opera House, Covent Garden. He admits that he initially had some misgivings about the proposed collaboration: 'I was introduced to Zandra Rhodes by Ian Campbell, who thought we might be a good team. I have to confess that I was slightly nervous. Of course I knew of Zandra and her work, but from a director's point of view half of the contribution to a production comes from the designer – not just in what a production looks like, but in what it says about the piece, the characters and the director's dramatic approach. So this would mean going into unknown territory for me with a first-time set designer and second-time costume designer.'

One of Ian Campbell's main reasons for involving Rhodes was the fact that the opera is set in Sri Lanka. He felt that the Asian motif running through it would be perfect for Rhodes's vibrant imagination. 'The first sketches confirmed that my instinct was right. Her flair for fabric and colour made it appear suitably exotic, while her innate taste ensured that this wasn't going to be a vulgar realization.' Campbell realized that Rhodes would, of course, require some technical support to develop her ideas. 'But to have her mind's eye on all aspects of the opera's visual side would ensure an integrated whole, and a colour palette that would blend costumes and sets harmoniously and would otherwise be difficult to guarantee.'

Another reason in favour of the collaboration was Campbell's confidence that Rhodes could work within the confines of the production budget – this time $300,000 for

> **❝** I used some bits of my prints, plus fabrics from nearby small towns on the Mexican border and some from a pile of old ethnic cushions…all sorts of mad things.

the sets and $165,000 for the costumes. Neither he nor the director wanted an expensive, 'over the top' staging. The production was also to travel to other theatres, so a certain degree of flexibility was required. Campbell and Sinclair asked for a set painted on soft cloth so that it could be adjusted to suit the various venues to which it would travel. 'There were some props in masonite, but most of the set was stretched-out canvas,' explains Rhodes. 'If the stage in question was two metres smaller on each side, then the canvas could just be rolled up.'

Rhodes is quick to praise her collaborators at the San Diego Opera. 'I was amazed at how much the team cooperated with me. They would always tell me if this or that didn't quite work.' She learned that it is wise 'to find out as soon as possible what the lighting is going to be like', adding that, memorably, in David Hockney's production of *Turandot* the lighting was 'out of this world'. Rhodes also proved to be adept at assimilating information. As Andrew Sinclair comments, 'She's a very clever woman, who researches thoroughly – she actually went to Sri Lanka – and listens to the music all the time while working. She said, "Just tell me if you don't like something and indicate what you want, because this is new to me."'

In set construction Rhodes was guided by John David Peters, the head of the Technical Department at San Diego Opera, as she needed help with the way her designs were to be realized on stage. 'I guess what Zandra discovered from the set design process,' he says, 'was how minimal you can be in what you put on stage. She began by presenting me with some very literal set designs and gradually, over a series of meetings, we just took away items.'

Rhodes realized that realistic drawings were not what the team at San Diego expected from her. 'If they wanted that, they could have gone to someone within the operatic circuit. I think they came to me for the Zandra Rhodes imagination and vision of things. As Ian pointed out to me, Bizet had never been to Sri Lanka – or to Spain for his *Carmen*, for that matter. He'd never seen the place. Originally the story was going to be set in Mexico, which he hadn't seen either! So the whole thing is about imagination, about Zandra Rhodes's take on the story, i.e., something exotic.'

Andrew Sinclair explains that, 'In the end it boiled down to what we wanted to say about the piece, which is a difficult one for a director – beautiful music, weak libretto. I was keen to play as much as possible of what we could get from the libretto to make this opera a dramatic piece with believable characters, i.e. to play the conflict that occurred before the opera begins. The music is lush and exotic, but there is also a tribal, almost primitive element in the story. To try and convey this, I had already decided there would be more dance in this production than just the set pieces. So we needed a clear stage for dance, and we needed a production that would be attractive for other companies to hire (which they have), and not too unwieldy scenically (the entire production fits in one transport wagon). It was important that we presented what Zandra could bring to the piece – a wonderful sense of colour, texture and fabric. So in the end the set design was quite easy.'

Rhodes comments that she found it 'a wonderful experience' and 'loved every minute of it'. As she recalls: 'The workshop of the technical department was in a dilapidated building in a rough downtown area, where they build scenery and props for theatres all over America. Their team started work at 7.30 am and were great to work with.' Here Rhodes learned some of the technicalities of stage design, such as the fact that it has to be *bold*. The team would translate her sketches and ask whether she liked this or that interpretation. 'I would then look at them and either say yes or make adjustments. I had a wonderful English second-in-command on the technical side, who had to work out how things would roll on and fit together, and how the set changes would work out.'

Campbell recalls that the workshop equally adored working with Rhodes, who 'taught as much as she learned, leaving the team with some new ideas they will utilize for years to come, and it was done with such affection and humour that no one could ask for more'. Rhodes recalls an example: 'In the opening scene, the action takes place on a sunny, sandy beach; then a storm has taken place, so the set is grey and dreary, and the singers are standing and moving on rain puddles. We devised a floor made of cloth, which at the beginning had to be hammered down. For the opening scene, on the sunny beach, a yellow layer went on top of that. Simple! So, when halfway through the opera you have the storm, all you needed to do was remove the yellow layer and, at a stroke, you had the setting for the second half. For economy's sake, they didn't want to have to paint the floor all over. As I'm also a textile designer, I could devise a format for them that *looked* as if the whole floor was painted over. But in fact, it consisted of 3-foot-square panels, which were stencilled individually and then stuck together. That saved them a great deal of time and money.'

Andrew Sinclair confirms that he, too, learned from Rhodes and recalls the day she took him into her studio to show him some ideas for palm trees. 'I can sometimes be a fairly conservative person. I was confronted by these towering, tracing-paper prototypes in pink, orange and vivid red. My immediate reaction was, "Whoa!" But then I settled down and looked at them and they said the very things we wanted to convey about the beach scenes – exoticism and heat. And that's how they exist in the production.'

For the costumes Rhodes used cheap polyester saris, which she got at a market just outside Los Angeles. She brought them back to her studio in London, where she printed

ABOVE Sketch of a costume for Radames, the young general who is the object of the affections of both Princess Amneris and her slave Aida, for a production of Verdi's *Aida* that originated at Houston Grand Opera in 2007 before travelling to the English National Opera and the San Francisco Opera.

over them and, as she put it, 'Zandra-fied' them. After a trip to India, she went back to San Diego and worked on the wigs and make-up, so that they could be made to look as South Asian as possible.

As Sinclair noted: 'It was also helpful that, spending half of each month in California, Zandra was able to work closely with the choreographer, John Malashock, to decide what would and wouldn't work in terms of fabric and masks for the dancers. A particular gift of Zandra's as a costume designer has always been a keen awareness of singers' needs. She has supervised the production everywhere it has gone, changing things to suit various singers – covering them up or uncovering them, depending on physical suitability; changing wig styles; or just adding things. Just as I try and do something new each time the production is presented, so Zandra likes to keep her side of the production fresh.'

The work is so cleverly packaged that it has been able to travel all over North America, including Michigan, San Francisco, Miami, Denver, Minneapolis and Montreal. In fact, at the biennial meeting at which all the North American opera houses display their wares, the management of the Montreal Opera announced that they loved Rhodes's input into *The Pearl Fishers* so much that they would have taken San Diego's *Magic Flute*, too, if Michael Hampe's production had had sets as well as costumes by her.

By the time Rhodes came to design her third opera, *Aida*, for the Houston Grand Opera, English National Opera and San Francisco Opera (2007), she had discovered that 'you have to spar a little with each director, and see how you can come to a solution that fulfils both your visions, although the overall concept of the production is always theirs'. Jo Davies, who directed all three stagings, explains that the project was put together by John Berry, Artistic Director at the ENO, and Anthony Freud, General Director at Houston, 'who were looking for a co-production of *Aida* that would be planned very much around Zandra. This is the other way round from the usual process of planning a production, when the *director* usually chooses his designing team. They asked me if I could meet Zandra and see if we could deliver such an *Aida*. So we met in London. Meanwhile, she had been working on the sets with a technical director in Houston, and had put together a model which was based on huge pieces of scenery that couldn't be moved or shifted between scene changes without bringing down the curtain for several minutes. But technical problems can easily be fixed and, as the images themselves were fantastic, I said yes right away. The spirit of her designs was very much in keeping with what Verdi wanted. In his notes, he asked for colours that are bright and rich and splendid. He wanted a vibrancy and exoticism that are perfectly matched by Zandra's designs. The more I read about Egypt, the more I discovered that some of the aspects of the libretto were historically impossible. For instance, the Egyptians never worshipped Vulcan – he was a much later, Roman god. So what Verdi was creating was an artist's impression of Egypt. And Zandra perfectly matched that.'

The highly 'exotic' *Aida*, which Verdi composed for the opening of the Suez Canal in 1871, is ideally suited to a large stage, but within this broad canvas, it also contains an intense, intimate drama, which takes place between the four main characters. Aida, slave of the Pharaoh's daughter, Princess Amneris, is herself an Ethiopian princess, and she shares her mistress's passion for the young Egyptian army commander Radames, who is in turn in love with Aida but is chosen to lead the Egyptian army's attack on her country. Her vanquished father, Amonasro, the Ethiopian king, hopes to use Aida's and Radames' love for each other to discover the route the Egyptians will take for their attack on his

ABOVE Sketch for the Ethiopian princess-turned-slave Aida in the Triumph Scene of the eponymous opera. Turquoise, gold and ultramarine proved key colours in Rhodes's palette for the production.

country. The danger that the larger-than-life background to the opera might be allowed to overshadow the inner drama must be carefully averted.

Jo Davies's view of the principal female characters is that 'Aida is quite interesting in terms of character and psychology. She is a slave in the Egyptian court, a displaced person, clearly out of her natural environment. But because of her princely heritage, she remains very strong and individual, with a boldness that comes with hereditary right. Considering her position, she stands up to Amneris with great vigour and honesty. She is a very true and noble spirit, and this is what irritates Amneris, who, despite her power, lacks that nobility of character. She is simply used to having anything she wants and refuses to accept that there is anything – in this case, Radames – that she can't have. She tries to set Aida and Radames against each other and, in the Judgment Scene, oscillates between obsession and threats. Throughout the opera, she either barks and shouts or pretends to be incredibly nice to somebody, which – as we see in Act I, Scene II, where she traps Aida into revealing her love for Radames – is when she's at her most dangerous. There is a nobility and grace in Aida that is totally lacking in Amneris, and I am sure that this is what Radames connects to.'

❝ I took a very colourful view of Egypt, based on some of my personal sketches and on some of Napoleon's Egyptian campaign etchings – translated into very bright colours: turquoise, gold, ultramarine, orange.

Of Radames, Davies notes: 'He doesn't know that Aida is a princess; he thinks she is a slave. In ancient Egypt, any relationship other than rape between a slave and an Egyptian was punishable by death – of the slave, that is. So what Radames has to do in order to marry Aida is to gain her liberty. This is what he is dreaming about in his opening aria, "Celeste Aida", and this freedom for all Ethiopian slaves is what he claims after his victorious campaign. He knows that, having won this great victory, he can claim anything he wants, and that if Aida is no longer Amneris's slave, they can get married. Aida is also anticipating that, if he returns from the war victorious, they can marry.

'The psychological turning point in the opera is when, having first granted Radames his wish to free the Ethiopian slaves, the Pharaoh publicly offers him his daughter Amneris's hand in marriage, when all he had been fighting for throughout the campaign was to come back and marry Aida. But the Pharaoh's offer is made in such a public, "political" way, if you like, that it becomes a command from which he cannot escape – which is why he later arranges to meet Aida in secret, by the Nile. But the difficulty in putting across this crucial turning point, and the reason why it's so often overlooked, is that it happens in the middle of the Triumph Scene, with huge crowds of people moving about. But I am sure that Verdi did this deliberately. He intended to indicate the interplay between political and personal affairs, the fact that the feelings and aspirations of the protagonists are lost in state affairs. The psychology of each of the characters is very solid, but they are all pawns in the political power game. That's why he interposes political power scenes – be they of the Throne or the Temple – between the intimate scenes.'

ABOVE Sketch for the costume of Princess Amneris's father, the Pharaoh of Egypt, from *Aida*. The triangular shape of the skirt is a repetitive element in the costumes and also in the set designs, emphasizing the love triangle around which the opera takes place.

OPPOSITE Sketch for one of Aida's costumes. Rhodes was inspired by the Tuareg people of North Africa for Aida's facial decorations.

Rhodes thoughtfully interpreted sets and costumes in line with Davies's concept. 'I took a very colourful view of Egypt, based on some of my personal sketches, done back in 1985, and on some of Napoleon's Egyptian campaign etchings – translated into very bright colours: turquoise, gold, ultramarine, orange. I visualize Aida herself as smouldering. She must exude sexuality. She must look "civilized" and, at the same time, "ethnic". I based her make-up on Tuareg faces – an ethnic touch, so that she doesn't look Egyptian. Princess Amneris is tortured and spoilt. She must have regal presence, and my job is to make the diva feel and act *thinner*! Radames is ambitious and conscious of being head of the Egyptian army. He must look handsome – whatever his build – and *believable*. Amonasro, the warrior king of Ethiopia and Aida's father, has to look handsome and, like her, "ethnic". I printed my African zebra print on brown suede to hang across his body, and used rough paintwork on ethnic-style fabric for trousers, etc.'

Rhodes's initial concept was that, as in original Egyptian tomb paintings and papyri, the women would go bare-breasted. 'My idea was that they would wear flesh-coloured body stockings tightly stretched so that you wouldn't get any wrinkling. This is quite common practice, because most opera singers don't like having their arms bare, so they usually wear a transparent fabric over them, as do most people in show business, including ice skaters. This fabric would make the cast look as if they were naked, with their armlets and bracelets made of a stick-on fabric that looks like brocade. My idea was to have those flesh-coloured body stockings and then paint the nipples and the accessories on. There was no way I would have them go around stark naked…but the people at Houston said that because Texas was part of the Bible Belt, they couldn't envisage them even *looking* naked on stage. So I had to raise the body suits to cover their breasts. This was a compromise…. The materials were polyester because it pleats beautifully, the pleats never come out, and pleated polyester is then washable. The collars were beautifully made – of leather and raised acrylics.' Rhodes explains that when there are cast changes or the production travels to new theatres, the only things that need to be altered are the costumes of the main characters, which can be adjusted according to sizes and shapes, and changed in minor ways the singers might ask for, 'because they have to feel happy in their costumes so that they feel free to sing beautifully'.

Jo Davies was more than satisfied with the costumes Rhodes produced on her budget of $250,000 for sets and costumes and $50,000 for props. The practicalities of the staging, however, were another matter. 'I remember having to ask where the king and seventy-five other people were supposed to enter from! The technicalities – all those matters relating to space, and the psychology of space, and the connection of the audience to each character in each scene – were things that Zandra had to learn. The process was daunting at first. We had more discussions about things like that than about the costumes!'

While Rhodes was rehearsing in Houston, Anthony Freud mentioned that he could imagine her doing a production of *Turandot*. Would Rhodes like to have a go at Puccini's 'Chinese' opera, and does she have any unfulfilled dreams as far as the operatic stage is concerned? 'Opera as an art form is like "the sky's the limit",' she replies. 'You can't go any higher or any better than that. I hope that some director, somewhere, will think of me and propose some future collaboration. Then I'll listen to the music, imagine it in visual terms, and produce my own version of what it should look like!'

PAMINA

Daughter of Queen of the Night

fabulous sheer fabric

Egyptian star print
delicate, gorgeous stars

OPPOSITE Sketch for Pamina's costume in *The Magic Flute*, mirroring the innocence of this young and idealistic character.

ABOVE Prince Tamino (John Osborn) plays his magic flute, which bewitches even the wildest of animals and makes them dance. The animals were made in London, while the monkey costumes, worn by actors, were made in San Diego.

LEFT The Queen of the Night (Cui Yan-Guang), descending in a spectacular, starry costume and an equally spectacular, elaborately constructed set made – at Rhodes's suggestion – to look like the night sky.

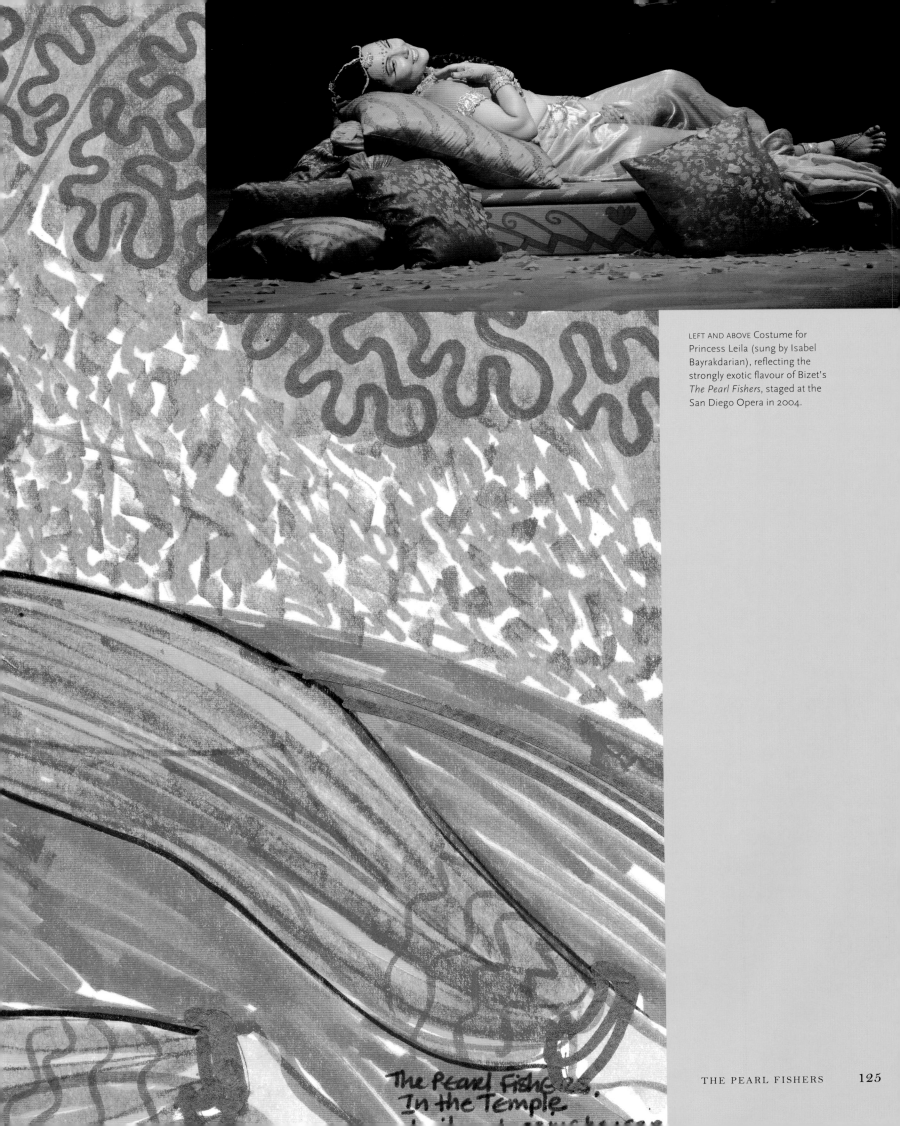

LEFT AND ABOVE Costume for Princess Leila (sung by Isabel Bayrakdarian), reflecting the strongly exotic flavour of Bizet's *The Pearl Fishers*, staged at the San Diego Opera in 2004.

The Pearl Fishers.
In the Temple

THE·PEARL·FISHERS
Dancing maidens on the Beach.

glittering black
base with mirrors
mirrored nostrils
and mirrored eyes.

Coloured beadwork.
glitter & irridescent
on the fabric mane.

OPPOSITE Sketch for temple
dancers. The squiggles
shown in the sketch are
Rhodes's signature motif.

RIGHT Sketch for a temple
dancer's 'animal' costume,
with horsehead mask.

THE PEARL FISHERS.
Dancer in Horsehead mask.

AIDA

RIGHT The Triumph Scene in *Aida*, as staged at the English National Opera, 2007. To the left of Princess Amneris, the Pharaoh and Radames are the priests, whose pleated skirts are supported by crinolines and whose bare chests are, in fact, body stockings with nipples painted on.

ABOVE In Act I Scene II, Amneris (Jane Dutton) tricks Aida (Claire Rutter) into revealing her love for the young general, Radames, who is also loved by Amneris. Rhodes used henna for additional arm decorations, as real armbands would rattle distractingly.

OPPOSITE Sketches for various characters in *Aida*, a highly populated opera. Pleated dresses and skirts were a central element of the costumes. Rhodes used polyester fabrics in order to keep the pleats in place.

mum low bust.

glittering breast plate with eye

pleating knotted into dramatic pyramid shape

❝ Aida is interesting in terms of character and psychology: a slave in the Egyptian court, a displaced person, clearly out of her natural environment. But because of her princely heritage, she remains very strong and individual, with a boldness that comes with hereditary right. JO DAVIES, DIRECTOR

LEFT Sketch of a costume for a guard in the Nile Scene (Act III) and the Judgment Scene (Act IV). The Egyptian eye (seen here on the breastplate) and the pleating knotted into a dramatic pyramid shape were central motifs in the costumes and the staging.

BELOW Another view of the Triumph Scene, with Radames (sung by John Hudson) riding in on a giant elephant fashioned out of blue silk, covered, like the Pharaoh's robe, in Rhodes's trademark squiggles in gold.

ABOVE AND BELOW In the Judgment Scene, Princess Amneris (Jane Dutton) begs High Priest Ramfis (Matthew Best) to spare the life of Radames, whose capture she has caused but with whom she is hopelessly in love. Rhodes designed a magnificent bird-like costume for the priest to wear.

BELOW CENTRE AND RIGHT Sketches of two costumes for Princess Amneris. According to Rhodes, the character must have 'regal presence'.

Emanuel Ungaro

'I love music so much that I always dreamed of working in the opera'

When he was still at the helm of his eponymous fashion house, Emanuel Ungaro was often to be seen – a highly attractive man in a pristine white couturier's coat (reminiscent of a doctor's), with an ancient Egyptian amulet hung around his neck – either sketching furiously at his desk or, mouth full of pins, fitting and draping gorgeous fabrics around mannequins. Whatever he was doing, it was always to a background of operatic music.

Ungaro's passion for opera was so well-known in the *métier* and the circles around haute couture that the legendary conductor Herbert von Karajan once asked him to design costumes for his Salzburg production of *Otello*. Regretfully, Ungaro had to decline, as in those years he couldn't afford to take time off from his work as a couturier. He also declined an invitation from the Vienna State Opera to create costumes for the ballet *Scheherazade*, this time for a different reason: 'After Bakst, who would possibly want to dare to attempt *Scheherazade*?'

It was not until three decades later, in 2009, four years after retiring from his *maison de couture*, that Ungaro finally came to design costumes for the opera – and not for any old opera house, of course, but for no less an institution than the historic Teatro San Carlo in Naples, Europe's grandest, oldest (35 years older than La Scala) and (along with La Fenice in Venice) most beautiful opera house.

The invitation took Ungaro completely by surprise. 'I was on a train to Aix en Provence, when I suddenly received a call from the *commissario* assigned by the Italian Ministry of Culture to oversee the restoration and refurbishment of the San Carlo that was being carried out at the time.' Ungaro later found out that one of his wife's relatives, who was working at the San Carlo, had told her colleague about Ungaro's retirement from the couture and his passion for opera. The commissario had asked, 'So, why doesn't he come and do some costumes for us?', to which the relative had quipped, 'Why don't you ring and ask him?' So the commissario did just that.

He initially asked Ungaro to consider a production of *Faust*. Thinking that he was referring to Charles Gounod's opera, which has dozens of characters on stage – choristers, soldiers, labourers, students, and so on – Ungaro recoiled in horror. But upon learning that the reference was to *La Damnation de Faust* by Hector Berlioz, one of his favourite composers, he heaved a sigh of relief and felt confident enough to accept. 'For a start, the work has only three characters – Faust, Marguerite and Mephisto. Secondly, it's more like a "favola in teatro" than an opera, and therefore a less daunting challenge for a first-time costume designer.' In addition, the director was to be an old acquaintance, Jean Kalman, one of the world's most distinguished lighting engineers, who, years before, had created the lighting for one of Ungaro's shows. As Kalman happened to live in Paris, 'easy, constant and friendly' contact was possible between the two.

OPPOSITE Sketch for Berlioz's *La Damnation de Faust* at the historic Teatro San Carlo in Naples, 2009. The sharp suiting carries here a threatening connotation.

Ungaro was already a fan of *La Damnation*, which he had seen in Luca Ronconi's magnificent production for Turin's Teatro Regio (1992), later brought to Paris with the superlative Belgian bass-baritone José van Dam in the role of Mephisto — Ungaro's favourite of the three main characters in the work. 'He is the only one who is very well defined and decisive in his attitude and actions. He knows his role in the scheme of things, and he knows exactly what he's after — Faust's soul. The other two characters are weak and allow themselves to be manipulated.' Does Ungaro understand and sympathize with Faust's weakness in yearning to be young again? 'I understand it, but I deplore it! This being, who is resigned and submissive — even in Goethe's play, on which Berlioz's work is based — embodies a panoply of interweaving feelings that are quite nebulous and complicated. There is this love for Marguerite, which is not really love but a sort of infatuation with a mirage, an image of Marguerite that Mephisto dangles before him. To express this fragility, and a certain poetic, illusory dimension that is part and parcel of the character, I dressed the tenor José Bros in a long, kaftan-ish robe. I did the same for Mephisto, who was sung by the famous Uruguayan bass-baritone Erwin Schrott, but in his case it was made of a very stiff, structured fabric with metallic stripes, and I also gave him a black leather mask, which I think was effective. He brought Orpheus to my mind, in the sense that he is an allegorical character, a being who exists outside time.

'Marguerite was sung by the Italian mezzo, Sonia Ganassi, who had a beautiful voice but was three months pregnant. Kalman wanted to place her in a high tower and have her sing from there, but she refused. So, being an inventive and versatile artist, Kalman invented a silent character, whom we dressed as a sort of Ophelia, with a veil, and whom he placed in the tower. While Ganassi sat on a chair on stage and sang, the actress in the tower mimed the role and made all the gestures, as if she were Marguerite. This gave the heroine another dimension, especially as she is a character who imagines herself to be someone else, another version of herself.'

Ungaro admired the San Carlo's artistic team for their daring decision to stage this particular work. He notes that 'basically there are two kinds of operas: those, such as this, which are open to various interpretations, and those, such as Mozart's *Le nozze di Figaro*, which are cast in iron and cannot be played around with, and, if you do, it makes no sense.' Of *La Damnation*, he comments, 'It is a nebulous sort of work, in which nothing is clearly defined. This leaves the door open to many different interpretations. Unfortunately, it also leaves it open to all sorts of exaggerations.' He had nothing but praise, however, for Kalman's production, 'with its extreme clarity, simplicity and fantastic aesthetic sense.

'From the technical point of view, as a costume designer, you have total freedom as far as fabrics and other materials are concerned. The important thing is that you be at the service of the music and the director.

This is your role in the theatre: to follow the road indicated by the director and, of course, to enrich the message of each composition, as the music is the be-all and end-all of any operatic production. As a couturier, I had total, absolute freedom. There were no restrictions whatsoever; nothing to respect, except a personal concept of aesthetics and ethics. But, as a costume designer, you have to respect not only the director's vision but also the singers, who have very specific roles, who sing very specific notes and words, and whose characters stand for very specific things. So you are enclosed within confines from which you cannot escape, a little like being in a cage. You are there to help the singers express, through your costumes, the characters they have to interpret on stage. And you must do it with modesty and humility.'

Ungaro's contribution to *La Damnation* was deemed so successful that he was immediately invited back to the San Carlo the following season, for a production of Mozart's last opera, *La clemenza di Tito*. This was to be premiered in 2010, directed by Luca Ronconi, the Italian director Ungaro had so admired years earlier. *La clemenza* is an 'opera seria', based on Racine's *Bérénice*, with an unexceptional libretto inspired by the famous Italian poet and librettist Metastasio but not actually written by him. (Ungaro notes that, in his opinion, the libretto of *La clemenza* is far inferior to that of Mozart's *Idomeneo*, an opera for which the designer has a true passion.)

Ungaro began preparations by visiting Ronconi at his home in Perugia. There, the director explained what he wanted to do and how he viewed the main characters: the Roman emperor Tito, and Vitellia, who aspires unsuccessfully to be Tito's empress and is in turn loved by one of his closest friends, Sesto. Ronconi placed the emphasis mainly on the characters' sentimental and amorous relationships. 'In Tito's case, for example, I was interested in highlighting how his lovelorn suffering at [his beloved] Bérénice's departure resulted in a different appraisal of the exercise of power.

'I proposed the end of the eighteenth century as a reference point, but viewed very freely through the fashions of the twentieth century. As far as the costumes were concerned, my only specific request was that Ungaro pay great attention to the male costumes of Sesto and Annio, who are sung by female singers, though I wanted him to avoid "masculinizing" their costumes.'

Naturally the theatre had 'incredibly little money', so Ungaro approached the old suppliers to his couture house, and they gave him the fabrics. 'I used lots of velvet, because it reflects light very beautifully, plus taffeta, both in a fantastic palette of colours. Even those with a walk-on part wore velvet jackets. As I was fully aware of the fact that singers can get very hot on stage, I used very light, unlined velvet and asked them to tell me if they felt comfortable and could move about freely. Basically, costumes feel hot only if they are ill conceived and/or badly fitted so that they render movement difficult.'

There were also other challenges to be faced. Ungaro recalls that, during their discussions, Ronconi omitted to mention that he wanted to include a group of *pretoriani* (imperial guards). Eventually their costumes had to be devised at extremely short notice. 'Inventing on the spot is not a problem,' says Ungaro. 'I used to do it all the time as a couturier. But all of a sudden Luca decided that he wanted these guards to sport eyecatching breastplates! Now, making dozens of breastplates in metal is not exactly simple. So, having located an artisan in Naples, I had them made in leather. I was inspired by Titian's famous painting of Emperor Charles V, in which he wears a magnificent breastplate. For a note of modernity, I paired the breastplates with parachutists' trousers and military boots.'

The greatest difficulty Ungaro encountered was neither the meagre budget nor having to invent on the spot, but the fact that he had to conceive the costumes for singers he had never set eyes on, either in the flesh or in pictures. He was simply sent a list of names, with vague measurements, so had to design 'blind'. 'Naturally I knew the charac-

> ❝ On one hand I had my sketches and the ideal vision of the characters, and on the other I had blunt reality, which had nothing to do with my dream vision of the characters.

ters these singers were going to interpret, but I had no idea of the shape or size of their bodies, not even a photo. Evidently I had to try the costumes on a model to work out the proportions. So, on one hand I had my sketches and the ideal vision of the characters they expressed, and on the other I had blunt reality, which had nothing to do with my dream vision of the characters. So I was faced with huge surprises! In the event, Tito was sung by Gregory Kunde. Vitellia was sung by a young Roman soprano, Teresa Romano. I gave her a jewel to wear, a spider's web that symbolized the fact that she is at the centre of this huge web of intrigue. Although it couldn't be seen very clearly from afar, to me it symbolizes the essence of this character. Sesto was sung by Monica Bacelli, a mezzo with a voice of extraordinary beauty, who delivered a very fragile, very moving portrayal of this character, my favourite in the opera. But Sesto was shorter than Servilia, sung by Elena Monti, a young but extremely tall soprano, about one metre eighty, who towered above him! When Ronconi saw Servilia in costume, he exclaimed: "But you managed to make her look so light and airy! How did you manage to do that?"'

Ungaro reckons that the fact that he was a couturier rather than a trained theatrical costumier helped a great deal because 'for all classical couturiers, a sketch is but an idea, a departure point, which often has little to do with the completed outfit that appears on the runway. The sketch is transformed, with imagination, by the dictates of the fabric, and, in this case, the shape and personality of each singer. I was amused that Ronconi, used to theatrical costumiers, would sometimes remark, "But on your sketch there was a button here.

OPPOSITE Sketch for Vitellia in Mozart's *La clemenza di Tito* at the Teatro San Carlo, 2010. The director, Luca Ronconi, proposed the late eighteenth century as a starting point for Ungaro's designs.

Why isn't there one in the finished costume?" I replied that I couldn't be a prisoner of a sketch, even if it happened to be mine! I just improvised on many of the costumes, which were modified and made to measure and on the spot. Then Ronconi also asked, "But how will the conspirators look?", to which I would reply, "I don't know. We'll see. I'll improvise something." This is how I work. Even as a couturier, I never knew how a collection would end up, exactly. I drew sketches, more like "aide-mémoires" to myself than anything else. Then I worked all the shapes and details directly on the models. I never produced "concept" collections.'

Ungaro stayed in Naples for two whole months. He worked on each of the costumes himself, 'with pins and scissors', at the San Carlo's ateliers, because 'I wanted to live the life of the theatre fully. So, going to the San Carlo every morning was a treat in itself. I was there from nine in the morning until eight in the evening and this was pure bliss for me. I love music so much that I always dreamed of working in the opera sometime, ever since I had to refuse those invitations long ago.' Ronconi felt satisfied and vindicated in his choice: 'His costumes were indispensable elements in fulfilling my conception as a director. He was an excellent colleague, with whom I would welcome an opportunity to work again.'

Ungaro's love of opera dates back to his childhood. His father, a tailor with anti-fascist sentiments, had left his native village near Brindisi in Puglia during the Mussolini era and settled in Provence, where his six children were born. He happened to have a marvellous light-lyric tenor voice, slightly reminiscent of the Spanish tenor Alfredo Kraus, according to Ungaro, and ideal for Rossini. 'He knew every opera by heart and communicated his love to me. Our home was always, always flooded with music. His particular passion was *verismo*, and especially Puccini. Sometimes, when we were cutting jackets together in his atelier, we would start singing whole operas together, more often than not *La Bohème*, in which he, with his lighter voice, sang Mimì, while I, with my heavier tenor, sang Rodolfo.'

Apart from *Idomeneo*, which Ungaro says he has heard 'about six hundred times', his favourite operas include Alban Berg's *Lulu* (he saw the famous Patrice Chéreau/Pierre Boulez production three times) and the works of Richard Strauss, though above all the 'noir' Strauss of *Salome* and *Elektra*, in which the composer almost touches what Schoenberg was to develop later, before retreating to the 'pink' Strauss of his Viennese operas, which Ungaro is not particularly drawn to.

Does he ever miss fashion and the world of haute couture, where his clients included Jackie Onassis, Lauren Bacall, Catherine Deneuve, Anouk Aimée and the Duchess of Windsor? 'No, because the profession no longer resembles what it used to be. I came out of Cristóbal Balenciaga's world, and it has nothing to do with what goes on today. That world had a nobility, an aesthetic as well as an ethic, a moral stance and a discipline in the exercise of the profession. Balenciaga maintained that a good couturier must think of the architectural construction of a garment and also feel himself a poet, a painter, a musician and a philosopher. There was no frivolity. Nowadays fashion has changed completely. Everything is done for show, for publicity, and the market is dominated by large groups or conglomerates such as Zara, Mango, Uniqlo and companies who use clothes merely as pegs for their accessories. Having said that, I am not one of those who advocate that couture was ever an art form. It is too ephemeral for that. The aim of couture is to dress women. And, as Chanel used to say, we couturiers are not artists but artisans. Art is what one considers ugly today and beautiful tomorrow. Fashion is what one considers beautiful today and ugly tomorrow.

'As a couturier, all you might hope to do is leave behind some memories, some traits that might give some direction to fashion at some future point. But that's all. It's a very ephemeral profession and also a very cruel one, compelling you to expose yourself four times a year, and for that you need tremendous temerity. You also need some culture, something that I fear the young of today do not give themselves enough time for. Yet they must, they have to learn, whereas the duty of someone like myself, who had the good fortune to learn my craft from Balenciaga, is to try and transmit what I know. I'm certainly not taking it with me to the grave! But I'm not sure up to what point all this is of interest to the young designers of today, who tend to be very frivolous and superficial, and whose principal aim seems to be to behave like rock stars!'

Ungaro's own style as a couturier was dominated by an all-pervasive, refined sensuality that expressed itself in seductive, feminine clothes in fluid shapes, with a wonderful sense of colour and a unique way with prints, denoting a 'Mediterranean' man who truly loved women. 'Being French by birth and Italian by origin – and Pugliese, to boot, which means being practically Greek – I am lucky enough to benefit from these cultures.' Ungaro is also an avid reader of poetry and philosophy – 'I don't read novels any longer' – and an immensely gifted interior decorator, as both his homes testify.

So is he satisfied with life and his performance, so far, as costume designer for the opera? 'One is never fully satisfied. One would have to be an idiot to be that. One always feels there is something one could have done better, some detail that could be more refined, more elegant; exactly as one did when preparing a fashion collection, when one suddenly had the impulse to remove a sleeve, or change a shoulder, but it was too late, the models were already out on the catwalk. But, ultimately, yes. The point is that one doesn't do it for the money, or the glory, or whatever; one does it for love.

> **6 6** I gave Mephisto a
> black leather mask, which
> I think was effective…for
> an allegorical character,
> a being who exists
> outside time.

BELOW Sketch of a costume for Faust;
as Ungaro points out, 'a weak character
who allows himself to be manipulated'.

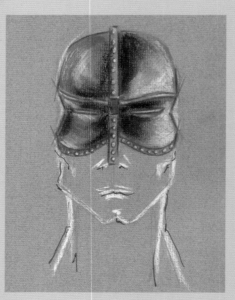

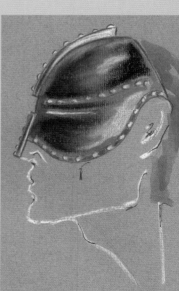

TOP Sketch of an eyecatching costume for
Mephisto, a well-defined character, decisive
in his attitude and actions, with the goal of
obtaining Faust's soul.

ABOVE Two sketches for Mephisto's black leather
mask. The studded trim gives the object a suitably
sinister aspect.

OPPOSITE Sketch for Faust's costume, consi
of a long, sweeping robe and a billowing,
detachable cape.

OPPOSITE AND RIGHT Tito
(sung by Gregory Kunde),
in *La clemenza di Tito*,
Teatro San Carlo, 2010.
The velvets for all the
costumes were provided by
the suppliers of Ungaro's
Parisian couture house,
which he sold in 2005.

OPPOSITE Sesto, the idealistic young hero (sung by Monica Bacelli), wears a printed jacket, knotted jabot and crushed velvet trousers. Ungaro heeded the director's exhortation that the costumes for Sesto and Annio, both sung by female singers playing male characters, should not be 'too masculinized'.

LEFT The scene portraying the burning of the Capitol. Even characters with walk-on parts wore splendid velvet jackets and silk trousers.

66 I was inspired by Titian's famous painting of Emperor Charles V, in which he wears a magnificent breastplate. For a note of modernity, I paired the breastplates with parachutists' trousers and military boots.

LEFT AND ABOVE Servilia (sung by Elena Monti) in embossed velvets that give a rich textural effect. All the velvet costumes used in the opera were light and unlined, so that the singers could move about freely.

OPPOSITE Vitellia (Teresa Romano), her dramatic costume enhanced by a spider necklace, which, to Ungaro, symbolizes the web of intrigue in which the character is embroiled.

RIGHT The commander of the imperial guards, Publio (Vito Priante), whose dark, austere costume mirrors the rigour of his character.

Gianni Versace

'My motto is: absorb everything. It helps!'

'I am not a costume designer in the classic sense, but I hope I bring something new to the theatre,' declared Gianni Versace shortly before the opening of John Cox's production of *Capriccio* at Covent Garden in January 1991. 'And I hope that my interest in the theatre brings a passionate undertone and makes my designs for real life richer and more spectacular.'

Versace, a widely cultured man and a voracious reader, was passionate about music in general, and opera in particular, from the time of his childhood. He grew up in Reggio Calabria, where he learned to cut and sew in his mother's busy dressmaking atelier, while listening constantly to opera. He moved to Milan, aged 22, and for several years worked as a designer in the prestigious ready-to-wear firms of Callaghan, Jenny and Complice, before opening his own eponymous firm in grand premises on Via de la Spiga in 1978. Despite his hugely successful career, vertiginously busy schedule and some of the superficial aspects that are part and parcel of the world of fashion, Versace found the time to pursue his cultural passions, to amass a dazzling art collection ranging from Old Masters to Andy Warhol in his palazzos in Milan and at Lake Como, and to build a vast reference library from which he drew inspiration and guidance for his designs, both for the stage and the catwalk. 'I use background knowledge in everything I do,' he explained. 'In fashion you have to think of today and the atmosphere and mood of real life. In the theatre, there are too many references to the past to cancel out.'

Versace's first foray into the theatre, in 1982, was the ballet *Josephslegende*, with music by Richard Strauss, choreography by Joseph Russillo and sets by the painter Luigi Veronesi, at La Scala – the beginning of his collaboration with this legendary theatre, which continued the following year with the ballet *Lieb und Leid*, set to music by Gustav Mahler, and soon included three operas: Donizetti's *Don Pasquale* in 1984, Strauss's *Salome* in 1987 and Manzoni's *Dr Faustus* in 1989. The latter two operas were staged by Robert Wilson, whose idea it was to commission Versace. The theatre immediately welcomed the suggestion. 'I think that Gianni brought to the designs a fantastic sense of theatricality,' says Wilson. 'We didn't talk about the production details so much, just the general concept. Gianni was free to come up with his own invention within the overall design structure. It was a true collaboration and a dialogue between us. He proposed ideas and I reacted to them. The designs changed as a result of this exchange.' Wilson also encouraged Versace to 'make the designs "bigger", because theatre is different from fashion; the scale is different'.

Versace learned that he had to view each opera in its totality. As he recalls: 'When I did *Salome* with Bob, I had a lot of problems re-thinking the costumes so that the opera wouldn't end up being just about the Dance of the Seven Veils.' He also had to learn one

ABOVE Sketch of a ballerina for Richard Strauss's *Capriccio* at San Francisco Opera and the Royal Opera House, Covent Garden, 1990–91.

of the basic rules of being a theatrical costumier, which every couturier who aspires to design for the stage must learn: to be prepared for all the unforeseen cancellations and cast changes to which the operatic world is prone. In this instance, the original Salome, Eva Marton, was indisposed and had to be replaced by Montserrat Caballé, who was double Marton's size. Versace therefore had to re-think the costumes and ended up draping the ample-sized diva in soft folds. 'But I learned that even in cases where the costumes don't need to be changed or re-thought, there must always be enough fabric in the seams for the costumes to be let out – and they should be dry-cleanable!'

Wilson's production of *Dr Faustus* caused a major sensation, in which Versace's sensuous costumes played a significant role. The über-sexy costumes in the famous Bordello Scene were the talk of the town for weeks. 'I wouldn't say that Gianni's idea for the Bordello Scene illustrated my own,' Wilson now says, 'rather it complemented it. It was a counterpoint to my stark, architectural stage element.' Versace explained that his inspiration had come from childhood memories of the local brothel in his home town in Italy. 'When we went to church every Sunday, my mother – in many ways an avant-garde woman – and my aunt would cover their eyes and mine every time we passed a certain house. When I was a little older, I realized it was a brothel, and of course my imagination ran wild! So when I came to do the Bordello Scene in *Dr Faustus*, I decided to design it as I had imagined that house as a little boy. I designed a beautiful palazzo, full of ravishing young beauties dressed in the height of fashion. So, you see, my motto is: absorb everything. It helps!'

❝ When I came to do the Bordello Scene in *Dr Faustus,* I decided to design it as I had imagined a brothel as a little boy. I designed a beautiful palazzo, full of ravishing young beauties dressed in the height of fashion.

Based on their two collaborations at La Scala, Wilson's verdict on Versace as a costumier is that he was 'a perfectionist, who paid meticulous attention to detail. His artistic integrity was matched by his open-mindedness. With Gianni, you felt you were truly part of a team. I would have loved to work with him again. I think he could have done a brilliant *Aida*, and would also have been a brilliant designer for *Lulu*.'

At around the same time as Versace was venturing into opera, he began a long, prolific collaboration with Maurice Béjart, one of the twentieth century's greatest choreographers. This lasted from 1984 until Versace's tragic death in 1997, and took in more than a dozen ballets, including *Dionysos* (1984), *Malraux ou la Métamorphose des Dieux* (1986), *Leda and the Swan* and *Souvenirs de Leningrad* (1987), *Pyramide* (1990), *Sissi, the Anarchist Empress* (1993, with Sylvie Guillem) and *Barocco Bel Canto* (1997). The two men evidently fired each other's imagination and became close friends. Béjart rhapsodized about his favourite costumier: 'Working with Versace means being rejuvenated by a year every day and feeling the germinator of future creativity which lifts us

ABOVE Costume created for the Bordello Scene in Giacomo Manzoni's *Dr Faustus* at La Scala, displayed at the 'Versace-Teatro' exhibition that took place at the Royal College of Art, coinciding with the London performances of Strauss's *Capriccio*.

from earth in a dance with the planets.' Versace, for his part, felt exhilarated by the chance to research every project and cross-fertilize. 'You can sing with designs on stage. I try to add another dimension to the production with the costumes.' He certainly brought to the role of costumier both his flair for the theatre and his experience of dressing real people. In fact, his appreciation of people and wider horizons was a crucial factor that drew him to the stage. 'No prisoner of fashion, me! If you are a prisoner of fashion, you cannot see what is around you. You must be a part of the whole picture.' By designing for the stage, Versace also energized himself for what is possibly a couturier's greatest challenge: inventing new trends and producing instantly covetable objects of desire four times a year, twice for the couture and twice for the ready-to-wear collections.

It was during the revival of La Scala's *Don Pasquale* in the early 1980s that the Greek Cypriot stage designer Angelos Angeli, then working at the opera house on a scholarship, first came across Versace. 'He was forever changing and improving details of his costumes to suit new casts,' Angeli recalls. 'I first set eyes on him when he walked into the auditorium at La Scala, dangling a pair of drop earrings for the protagonist Adina, and

❝ Never think twice about something that your eye and your instinct know better than your conscious self. Do it immediately, take the plunge right away, before others can.

saying, "Is nobody here capable of changing these earrings?", which he wanted in red. So I took them off him and fixed them, without knowing that this was Gianni Versace, who, as you know, was then considered a god at La Scala! But as a young Cypriot student, although I knew exactly who "Versace" was, I didn't as yet know him physically.' Versace appreciated Angeli's spontaneous readiness to fix a problem and soon asked him to become part of his firm as a specialist assistant for his theatrical work, starting with the ballet *Dionysos*, which he was preparing with Béjart. Because Angeli was there on a scholarship, La Scala was cagey about the idea. In a gesture typical of him, Versace offered to pay Angeli himself.

'Gianni was a very instinctive, very intuitive being, with a knack for choosing the right person for the right job. "Never think twice about something that your eye and your instinct know better than your conscious self," he used to tell me. "When you stop to think about it, others will pick up the vibration from the air. So, do it immediately, take the plunge right away, before they can." He was a supremely gifted and very charismatic man, who knew how to capture the pulse of the moment, who knew his public, was often inspired by the street, and, being profoundly cultured himself, sensed and appreciated culture in others.

'He always told me that, coming from Calabria, a part of Magna Grecia, he always considered himself a Greek. And I was always amused by the fact that when he got really angry, he would instantly lapse into Calabrian dialect and only switch back to Italian when he had calmed down. That was his Instant Anger Management method.' Versace's Greek streak — also reflected in the Medusa design that became his firm's trademark —

meant that he felt particularly fired by the theme for *Dionysos* and produced a fantastic red costume, with pantaloons that opened up like zouaves, for the God character.

He also designed costumes for the Joffrey Ballet, Roland Petit and Zizi Jeanmaire (*Java Forever*), William Forsythe and the New York City Ballet (*Herman Schmerman*), and Twyla Tharp and the American Ballet Theater (*How Near Heaven*). The crowning glory of his theatrical career, however, was undoubtedly the production of Richard Strauss's *Capriccio*, directed by John Cox and shared between the San Francisco Opera, where it opened in October 1990, and the Royal Opera House, Covent Garden, where it opened in January 1991. It received a rapturous reception at both venues.

Typically, Versace re-thought and designed – mostly at his own expense – new, more sumptuous costumes for London than the ones he had prepared for San Francisco. These were inspired partly by Bakst's designs for Diaghilev's Ballets Russes, partly by Poiret's soft 1920s silhouettes, partly by the style of Coco Chanel (seen in the everyday costume of the actress Clairon) and partly by Sonia Delaunay's colourful geometric prints. The new costumes were made in exquisite fabrics and vibrant colours, and were full of 'couture' details such as bold, hand-embroidered motifs and jewelled cuffs. Janice Pullen, then Wardrobe Director at Covent Garden, remembers that 'Gianni very much enjoyed creating these costumes', which the director, John Cox, felt 'bordered on the miraculous'.

Speaking of the history of the staging, Cox comments: 'This was a very curious production, which has now become very hybrid. It started life thirty years ago at the Théâtre Royal de la Monnaie in Brussels, when Gerard Mortier, who was very design-driven, was General Director, and had sets and costumes by Mauro Pagano, who died two or three years later. As is often the case with productions, there were budget constraints, and the sensible thing to do, as far as the costumes were concerned, was to use the "design and hire" method. This means that you send the designs to a costume house like Tirelli in Rome, where they are made under the designer's supervision, then, when the production is over, they go back to the stock of that particular costume house. In this case, Brussels had arranged with Tirelli that the costumes would be available not only for the original run of the production at La Monnaie, but also for its revival a year later in Paris, as part of a co-production. Then, as is usual in such cases, they would form part of Tirelli's pool of costumes for hire.

'Much to my surprise, ten years after the production's first airing in Brussels, the Royal Opera House and Kiri Te Kanawa decided that they wanted to do this opera in London. Again, there were huge financial constraints and they really couldn't afford a new production. At the time I was Director of Productions at Covent Garden and they knew I had staged this work in Brussels. So they approached La Monnaie, whose administration said that Covent Garden could certainly buy the production, but warned that the costumes didn't exist any longer. Because Kiri had such strong ties with the San Francisco Opera, they agreed to a co-production, for which they would share all costs. So that's how this production came about.'

Since by now Mauro Pagano had died, a new costume designer had to be found. 'I decided to set the piece in the 1920s, the last heyday of the leisured classes,' Cox reports. 'As far as the set was concerned, some of the furniture was bought, some was made, some was hired – the usual dog's box! The Breakfast Scene looked very good, I thought. My concept was not that it should be an aggressively 1920s décor, but an inhabited country house in France, somewhere near Paris, where they would have some inherited family pieces mixed with some that were bought, and then add a couple of sofas to make things

ABOVE Sketch for a male dancer's arrival at and departure from the entertainment arranged by the Countess at her château in *Capriccio*.

comfortable, so that there was a real "English country house" atmosphere. There is something about French taste that has an eye for the English. One always sees copies of *Country Life* magazine on French coffee tables. So that was the atmosphere I was trying to create. Before doing the original production I was also a bit influenced by that movie, *Partie de campagne*.'

> ❝ I don't do costumes exactly as they were when the piece is set. There are people who do that much better than me. I do something different. I try to create something completely new.

While searching for a suitable costume designer, Cox realized that it might be a good idea to ask a couturier 'because couture fits into this sort of company very well…a very elegant company, where the characters are just the sort of people you would expect to be couture customers, people very aware of style, and with three heroines, each of whom would have a different idea of what constitutes suitable style. You have the Italian soprano, whose style is outrageous; the actress Clairon, with more classical taste; and, of course, the Countess, both more discreet and in her own home. So I thought it would be a great project for a spectacular fashion designer.'

What happened next was that Cox went on holiday to Greece and saw Béjart's company Ballets du XXème Siècle performing *Dionysos*, with costumes designed by Gianni Versace. 'I thought, here is someone who is not only a great fashion icon, but has also had theatrical experience, knows what a set looks like, and – which I didn't know yet – was an opera fanatic to boot! So, with Covent Garden's blessing, I got in touch with him and he agreed right away. After that, we were in constant touch. We had a proper working relationship, a lot of which was by post or fax, and lots of face-to-face meetings in London, in several other places and at his fabulous palazzo on the shores of Lake Como, where, having become very friendly, he invited me to stay a couple of times.

'As Gianni began to produce his ideas for the costumes, we both realized that the strength and direction of his designs wouldn't look that good against the existing furniture that made up the set. Because the costumes were so strong, the set needed to be more emphatic and more stylish. As there was no money for new furniture, Gianni suggested we reupholster it with loose covers in vivid red, which made it look more luscious. By this time, his role had changed. He was no longer just the costume designer; he was being an interior decorator plus! Nobody attempted to offer him an additional fee and he didn't have the crassness to ask for one. As the additions to the décor rather sharpened the problem of cost, he also paid for additional costumes, especially the female costumes, such as the Countess's final evening gown and Clairon's black-and-white "stage" dress, out of his own pocket. But in exchange, these remained his own property and, I believe, ended up in his museum.

'Personally, I always found him easily accessible and forthcoming with sketches, ideas, changes, adjustments, or anything else that was required of him. One of the few minor problems we had was arranging for Gianni to meet Kiri, who was singing all over the world (I had warned him about the fact that she was a more rounded beauty than his sketches seemed to take into account). Once, she was on safari in Africa and Gianni thought, "What next? She will be on the moon!"'

As far as the various characters were concerned, Cox's discussions with Versace were interesting because of the fact that the production pre-dated Versace's involvement, and he was coming to a staging that already existed. 'This meant that some of our ideas were very different. Because on one hand we had a production that worked very well, but on the other here was a designer, a major talent, moving in with me. It was like taking a new wife; something that changes the perspective and makes the kaleidoscope move. He made it particularly clear that, temperamentally, he wasn't interested in *verismo*, stark realism. He was interested in a strong, poetic feeling for the piece, which was absolutely fine by me. It seemed to me that everything he was introducing to the production suited the fact that we were now doing it in bigger theatres than before.'

Versace spent more than a year working on the designs and produced thirty-one different creations. Never partial to sketching, he preferred to mould his costumes on the human body, endlessly varying shapes and textures as he explored each character's true personality. 'I don't do costumes exactly as they were when the piece is set,' he remarked at the time. 'There are people who do that much better than me. I do something different. I try to create something completely new — as Bakst did for Diaghilev. People who go to the theatre either want to see a beautiful re-creation of the past, as with Visconti, or they want to see the avant-garde. I don't like anything in between.'

OPPOSITE The director John Cox transposed his production of *Capriccio* to the 1920s, but in order to keep a link with the opera's original eighteenth-century setting, asked Versace to design sumptuous crinolines for the stage play to be performed in the Countess's salon.

ABOVE In an unusual and brilliant initiative by John Cox, the musicians who feature in the opening scene of *Capriccio* were placed on stage, wearing eighteenth-century frock coats designed by Versace.

In their effort to make the piece more intense and poetic, Cox and Versace thought to give it back a hint of its original eighteenth-century setting. 'I had never done this before,' says Cox, 'but it seemed logical that when the actress Clairon comes to the château to rehearse the poet Olivier's new play, she would get into her costume and, at the end of the rehearsal, come to the drawing room still in costume so that the Countess can see it. This was the principal way of linking the two centuries.' This also explains the sensational crinoline in a geometric print worn by Clairon, in stark contrast to the 1920s influences that permeate the costumes worn by all the characters for their daily lives.

However, the most ambitious thing Cox has ever done with this piece — which he has directed several times before and since — is to have the opening sextet played, in full eighteenth-century costume, on stage rather than in the orchestral pit. 'We arranged the lighting so that the early twentieth-century furniture on stage was in darkness, while a funnel, or cone, of light fell on the eighteenth-century musicians' stands. And then, as the music faded away, the lights dimmed and the opera began to unfold on the main set.' Versace dressed the musicians in eighteenth-century frock coats in acid colours. Their waistcoats were jewelled and had luxurious, patterned linings, regardless of the fact that in costume design such detailing is rare.

Cox's transposition of the piece to the 1920s gave Versace the opportunity to draw on the Ballets Russes era for the dancers' costumes. The ballerina's tutu was made of five layers of different, densely patterned fabric, her tights were painted in wild, psychedelic prints, and she wore an oriental shawl around her shoulders. 'I worked for four months on that design — it has all the different patterns from Bakst's Ballets Russes,' Versace proudly explained. For Kiri Te Kanawa, who played the Countess, he designed possibly the most exquisite clothes ever to be seen on stage: a velvet coat, aptly described in the press as 'a waterfall of vivid pattern and rich texture', inspired by Paul Poiret and his fluid 1920s silhouettes; and, for the finale, a dreamy, embroidered gown that shimmered with every step she took. However, as wardrobe director Janice Pullen points out, 'The beads made it very heavy to wear. When it was not being worn, it had to be folded and packed, never hung.'

Te Kanawa's costumes are a prime example of Versace's flexibility and perfectionism. Originally, he had been warned that she preferred subdued colours and long sleeves. So he first went to San Francisco with trunks full of covered-up styles. But as soon as he saw the diva, he decided he had to change everything. 'She is so beautiful and tall,' he enthused in a newspaper interview, 'yet she was afraid of fashion. But she is happy now.' In San Francisco, in order to best suit her complexion, he had chosen light fuchsia for the more casual velvet outfit at her first entrance. For Covent Garden he created something totally different — a whole spectrum of red nuances (the use of vibrant colour alluding to the fact that *Capriccio* is not merely a comedy about the rival merits of words and music, but also an opera with passionate undertones), complete with fabrics and drapes ranging from velvet to heavy silks and satins. He also made a new beaded, embroidered sheath for the finale.

Te Kanawa enthused, 'That was definitely a couture dress I was wearing! I'd never worn clothes like that before, because I can't afford them. Do you realize how much those dresses cost? Gianni appreciated that the costumes moved out of his control once they got on stage. In San Francisco, we found that the train of the dress kept turning over as I moved around. Every time the sequinned train rolled over, it made a sound like a breaker on Malibu beach. I had to kick it flat surreptitiously with my foot. So Gianni re-lined it, but to no avail. Finally, in a solution typical of the theatre, the flooring of the entire stage was altered.'

Initially Janice Pullen had numerous misgivings about working with a couturier. '"What if someone cancels at the last minute and we have to fly someone in at three hours' notice?" "Have you put enough fabric in the seams for letting out?" "Will we be able to dry-clean the dress?" But Versace proved totally un-diva-like and cooperative. After all, he had had to deal with such problems before, at La Scala, early on in his career.' He was also willing to listen. '"Good point," he would say each time I made a valid suggestion.' His absolute willingness to change anything that could be bettered won him Pullen's unqualified respect. 'He never said, "That's finished!" Give him five minutes and he's changing

> ❝ People who go to the theatre either want to see a beautiful re-creation of the past or they want to see the avant-garde. I don't like anything in between.

something. As he usually got a downpayment for his work, his perfectionism meant that he ended up paying for these changes himself. But he certainly gave you something worth looking at.'

Not surprisingly, John Cox felt vindicated in his choice of Versace as costumier. 'The strength of Gianni's designs gave weight to this one-act comedy of manners. *Capriccio* tends to be an underrated opera, but Richard Strauss poured his own life experiences into what was to be his last composition. Any idea that Gianni's involvement was just a matter of designing the costumes, and that's it, is quite wrong. His input into the totality of the production was vital and a refreshing stimulus in a piece which I have directed many times.'

The London version of the production – which was accompanied by a major retrospective of Versace's theatre work, 'Versace-Teatro' at the Royal College of Art – was a major sensation and set the town abuzz. Scores of celebrities attended the premiere, including Versace's fellow designer Zandra Rhodes. Cox reminisces: 'The first night was a huge event. I remember dining with Joan Collins afterwards at the Ivy with Gianni and about twelve or fourteen more people. And – typical of the man and his generosity – when I told him I had a guest, he immediately suggested I bring them along, which made them agog with excitement. I still treasure the memories of our collaboration and still have a gorgeous cashmere sweater he gave me. I would have loved to work with him again… perhaps on some nineteenth-century work, because of his acute sense of drama and melodrama.'

❝ I had a lot of problems re-thinking the costumes so that the opera wouldn't end up being just about the Dance of the Seven Veils.

OPPOSITE Sketch for Richard Strauss's *Salome* at La Scala, Milan, 1987. The director, Robert Wilson, commissioned Versace because of his 'fantastic sense of theatricality'.

ABOVE Salome, when she first hears the voice of the Prophet Jokanaan (John the Baptist). Versace's costumes had to be bold in order to stand out in Robert Wilson's spectacular stage design.

RIGHT Sketch of a dress for *Salome*. The sexy, body-hugging design could easily have featured in any Gianni Versace couture collection.

& Versace was a perfectionist, who paid meticulous attention to detail. ROBERT WILSON, DIRECTOR

OPPOSITE ABOVE Scene from Giacomo Manzoni's *Dr Faustus*, premièred at La Scala, Milan, in 1989, with Robert Wilson's dramatic staging.

OPPOSITE BELOW Frau Schweigestill (Emma Papikian) stands out against a chorus dressed in minimalist monochrome. The character offers unconditional love to the hapless protagonist, Adrian Leverkuhn.

ABOVE Adrian Leverkuhn (sung by Marcel Vanaud), flanked by a dapper mime artist and the soprano Sylvia Greenberg in a striking veiled outfit.

RIGHT Sketch for a flamboyant crinoline-style dress with eyecatching headpiece.

ABOVE Sketches for the dancers, inspired by
Bakst's designs for Diaghilev's Ballets Russes

LEFT AND BELOW Sketches for the Countess's dress in the finale of *Capriccio* at San Francisco. According to Kiri Te Kanawa, the train of the dress made so much noise against the wooden floor of the stage that its design had to be modified for the opera's revival at Covent Garden.

RIGHT The Countess (Kiri Te Kanawa) wearing the spectacular beaded version of the costume – 'definitely a couture dress' – at Covent Garden.

ABOVE Sketch of Clairon's costume for her arrival at the château, before she changes into her 'stage' costume.

RIGHT The Countess (Kiri Te Kanawa) in her multicoloured velvet 'at home' coat, worn over a simple black dress.

Viktor & Rolf

'We are interested in things that don't necessarily go well together, such as a flower and a bomb'

One of the most delightful surprises of the 2009 Summer Festival season was Viktor Horsting and Rolf Snoeren's debut as operatic costumiers in Robert Wilson's production of Weber's *Der Freischütz* at Baden-Baden, one of Europe's newest, most exciting and most adventurous festivals. The Dutch duo's spectacular costumes, combined with Wilson's unique way with lighting and his abstraction of the work from naturalistic references, succeeded in creating a magical world with a dreamlike and surrealistic quality.

It was Wilson's idea to ask the design team known as Viktor & Rolf to collaborate on the production, after the three had worked successfully together on the ballet *2 Lips and Dancers and Space* for the Netherlands Dance Theatre. Wilson says of the duo: 'They are highly professional and understand theatre, colour, line, form and scale. I found the fact that this was the first time they were working on an opera refreshing.'

For their part, Viktor & Rolf accepted the assignment purely because the invitation came from Wilson. 'We didn't know opera at all. But the moment Bob asked, we immediately said yes. We did it solely out of admiration for him. We would have said yes regardless of which opera he proposed, be it Weber, Verdi or Puccini. When we worked with him on the small dance production in The Hague, we fell in love with his world. We can easily relate to his abstraction. Bob doesn't really work with stage designs, but mainly with light design.'

In an interview for the Baden-Baden Festival magazine, Viktor & Rolf confided to Rüdiger Beermann, Director of Public Relations, that when they collaborated with Wilson on the ballet, they were 'almost hypnotized by the magic way in which the costumes blended into his very personal universe. Something magical emerged from this union. Working with him is a dream. He manages to allow us total freedom, yet already knows exactly what he wants. He is courageous, uncompromising and authentic. These are traits we admire.'

Clearly, this was a case of genius meeting genius. The extraordinary talent of the hip but serious duo is evident in the technical mastery that enables them to bring to fruition – with a completely hands-on approach and an ever-present quirky sense of humour – their sometimes outrageous, yet always aesthetically stunning concepts. Wilson's genius, meanwhile, lies in the fact that he manages to free operas from their setting and render them timeless, thus getting to the core of their meaning without falling into what has become a cheap and atavistic (and often, on the director's side, purely narcissistic) habit of transposing them to another epoch. Wilson has often been quoted as saying that he hates naturalism 'because what is naturalistically produced on stage is artificial. The most difficult task is simply standing on stage. When this is done well, movement generates itself. Standing *is* movement! When you close your eyes, you hear

OPPOSITE Sewing on the thousands of Swarovski crystals that covered the costumes (here, Samiel's 'thunderbolt' outfit) in Carl Maria von Weber's *Der Freischütz* at Baden-Baden, 2009. The crystals were sewn on by hand in the opera-house workshops.

better. Or, conversely, when you switch off the sound on your TV set, you can follow movement better. And this is what I endeavour to convey to singers. Music does not need illustration, but a sort of anti-world. And so tension arises between stage and music. I don't explain to singers what they should think or feel, but I give them clear and formal instructions.'

As far as the costumes were concerned, Wilson gave Viktor & Rolf a brief description of each character and 'a short global mood of the opera'. Otherwise, as the designers recount, he left them 'completely free to come up with whatever we wanted. We e-mailed the designs to Bob, and he immediately loved them and gave us carte blanche to continue.

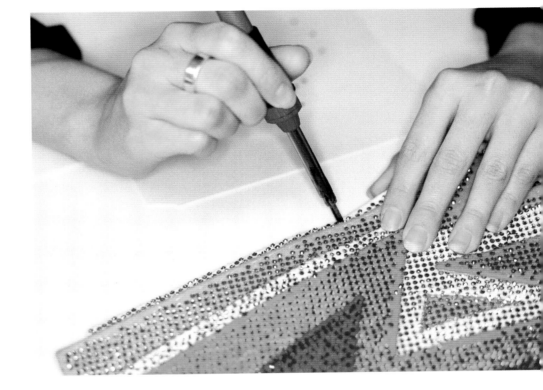

The beauty of Bob's productions is that his set design consists mainly of light. The lighting rehearsals take weeks, and this makes his productions very costly. But it places a lot of emphasis on the costumes; something that challenges us.' Light has always been the key element in Wilson's work. 'It is what helps us to see and hear better,' he explains. 'Without light, there is no space. I always start with light, as this is what creates shapes within space.'

Viktor & Rolf were also inspired by the fact that *Der Freischütz* is considered to be the first German romantic opera. 'We freely associated on the "German romantic" concept – a little Nymphenburg [porcelain], a little *Schwarzwald* [Black Forest]; something on the borderline of kitsch, but all completely open and twisted! We thought that if we could cover everything with crystals, this would capture Bob's magical light design and create a fairy-tale atmosphere. We wanted something sparkly, and so we contacted Swarovski to see if they were interested in participating.'

Swarovski certainly were. The finished designs, highly original and poetic, are worthy of a place in a costume museum. Male characters – including the hero, Max – were dressed as trees. The devil, in the guise of Samiel, wore an outfit depicting a thunderbolt. Women were transformed into flower bouquets, sprinkled or entirely covered with hundreds of crystals that twinkled and sparkled in Wilson's magical lighting.

The garment Viktor & Rolf devised for the opera's heroine, Agathe, broke new ground in costume design: a three-dimensional bouquet of huge, luscious, multicoloured flowers. The body of the soprano, Juliane Banse, was the stem, and her head another bloom. To obtain the three-dimensional effect, Viktor & Rolf mixed precious and 'poor' fabrics: organza, silk and satin with felt, Lurex and jute. Bows and ribbons with hand-lettering literally 'wrapped' the bouquet/dress. Like all the costumes, the dress was decorated in crystals from Swarovski's 'Crystallized' collection, laboriously sewn on by hand in the Baden-Baden wardrobe department.

Viktor & Rolf explain that one reason for asking Swarovski to get involved was that 'we wanted to avoid any sense of "reality" and were looking for an aesthetic that would underline the abstracted universe the characters inhabit. This was emphasized by suggesting that everything was touched by the same crystal stardust. Colourwise, in the first act, we didn't need to co-ordinate the costumes to the set. But in the last act, everything needed to be white. So we made the costumes return and repeat themselves in their "twin" white variation.' The men in the famous Huntsmen's Chorus were also dressed in white, with blond wigs and pointed red shoes.

Not surprisingly, both public and press were ecstatic about the costumes, and Viktor & Rolf received a standing ovation at the Baden-Baden Festspielhaus. The verdict of the local newspaper, the *Stuttgarter Zeitung*, was: 'Design is truly everything. Opera goes Fashion. An amazed whisper spread among the public as soon as new, spectacular costumes appeared – in delicate harmony with the music.' Bob Wilson was equally enthusiastic: 'They brought their own world to my world. The choice of materials was their own invention and a great complement to my scenic elements.'

How does being a duo function in terms of inspiration and practice? Does, for instance, Viktor create and look after certain parts of a project, while Rolf attends to others? Was the work for *Der Freischütz* divided between them, with specific areas allo-

❝ We didn't know opera at all. But the moment Bob asked, we immediately said yes. We did it solely out of admiration for him.… We were almost hypnotized by the magic way in which the costumes blended into his very personal universe. Something magical emerged from this union.

cated to each? 'No. Both on stage and in fashion we do everything together and there is no distinction between who does what.' Their ultimate surreal answer to the secret of their success is: $1 + 1 = 3$!

'As couturiers, the inspiration comes from fashion itself, from our lives, although, in our case, inspiration is never very literally translated into reality.' This may account for the fact that a surreal, kitsch or comic-strip element is often present, allowing the pair to bridge Baroque and Pop in a hitherto unseen way that is entirely theirs. It makes their sometimes very grand creations instantly contemporary (witness their stunning Spring 2010 tulle ballgowns, shorn unevenly in places), while some of today's more extreme trends are enhanced with their master-couturier scrutiny and cut. In the Festival magazine, they declared: 'Every creation of ours extends to a new borderline. We are interested in things that don't necessarily go well together, such as a flower and a bomb, for example.' (Their first – and highly successful – perfume was indeed named 'Flowerbomb'.)

Before the Baden-Baden assignment, Viktor & Rolf had collaborated with musicians such as Tori Amos and Rufus Wainwright (the latter attended the premiere at Baden-Baden). But their experience of opera amounted to nil, although, 'of course, we knew of the importance of opera in terms of culture'. After the *Freischütz* commission was confirmed, Bob Wilson took them to see Baz Luhrmann's production of *La Bohème* and

❝ We thought that if we could cover everything with crystals, this would capture Bob's magical light design and create a fairy-tale atmosphere. We wanted something sparkly, and so we contacted Swarovski.

Anthony Minghella's unforgettable staging of *Madama Butterfly* at the Metropolitan Opera in New York. Do they now listen to opera at work? 'No,' they reply. 'Listening to opera demands attentiveness and uninterrupted concentration. We would never play it as background music. Also the scenic aspect means a lot to us. We would only want to see opera live, in a theatre, so that we can savour the entire staging. Ultimately, we prefer to listen to music actively, to really pay attention. This requires a certain mood and we do that mainly at home.' In the design studio, 'we turn on the radio, just to generate energy in the room, but, if we need to concentrate, we work in silence'.

The duo enjoyed the experience of working on *Der Freischütz* and learned that 'as a creative discipline, inventing costumes for the stage differs from a fashion collection in the sense that fashion is an industry and the industrial process governs everything. Designing for the theatre is different and easier, because the parameters are purely artistic. There is no need for the costumes to function in reality. That is the difference between costume and fashion.'

Would they like to design another opera? 'Maybe, if the right plan comes along, together with the right director. We were once asked to do costumes for *Yolanthe*. It didn't happen, but we immediately had a beautiful concept and so we would love to do that one time.' What about a straight play, or a ballet? 'Sure. *Swan Lake* would be lovely. Or a musical...about ourselves!'

ABOVE Viktor & Rolf fitting the beaded thunderbolt onto Samiel's costume.

ABOVE The gamekeeper Max (Steve Davislim), in his costume depicting a tree, with fellow gamekeeper Kaspar (Dimitry Ivashchenko), whose soul is forfeit to the devil. They are seen here in the Wolf's Glen in Act II of *Der Freischütz*.

RIGHT Max's costume is lightly sprinkled with Swarovski crystals in order to enhance the director's light design and create a supernatural, fairy-tale atmosphere.

OPPOSITE ABOVE AND BELOW The demonic 'Black Hunter' Samiel (sung by Ronald Spiess) in his thunderbolt costume, with Max (Steve Davislim) in the Wolf's Glen.

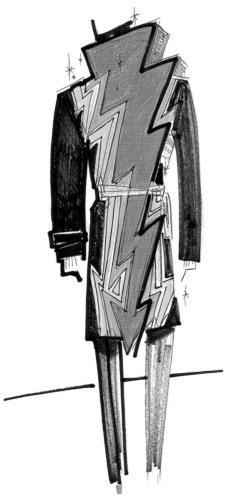

❝ We wanted to avoid any sense of "reality" and were looking for an aesthetic that would underline the abstracted universe the characters inhabit.

> **❝** We freely associated with the "German romantic" concept – a little Nymphenburg, a little *Schwarzwald*; something on the borderline of kitsch.

LEFT AND OPPOSITE The 11-kilo, multicoloured, three-dimensional 'Bouquet' dress, complete with bows and ribbons spelling out of the name of Agathe (sung by Juliane Banse), daughter of the head gamekeeper. The dress was made with a mix of precious and 'poor' fabrics, and decorated with Swarovski crystals.

OPPOSITE Agathe (Juliane Banse), wearing the white, 'twin' version of her multicoloured 'Bouquet' dress. Here, she kneels for her famous 'Prayer', the most beautiful aria in the opera.

ABOVE Agathe's bridesmaids in their eyecatching costumes. In the last act of the opera, key elements of the costumes reappear, now transformed from colour into white.

FOLLOWING PAGES The finale of *Der Freischütz*, with the hermit (Paata Burchuladze) granting Max absolution – the reason why all the costumes are replicated in white in the last act.

ACKNOWLEDGMENTS

The author wishes to thank the following people for their help in compiling the book:

Angelos Angeli

Count and Countess Jan d'Ansembourg

Maddalena Aspes, Press Office, Missoni, Milan

Pierre Audi, General Manager, Netherlands Opera, Amsterdam

Rüdiger Beermann, Director of Media and Communications, Baden-Baden Festival

Oliver Bezold, Press Office, Baden-Baden Festival

Vincent Boussard

Stéphane Bouteloup, Press Office, Monte Carlo Opera

Joseph Bradshaw, Watermill Foundation & Robert Wilson

Ian Campbell, General Director and Artistic Director, San Diego Opera

Valérie Caranta, Press Office, Opéra Toulon

Simona Chiappa, Prada, Milan

Eleonora Clapps, Press Office, Royal Opera House, Covent Garden

John Cox

Julia Creed, Photo Archive, Royal Opera House, Covent Garden

Jo Davies

Maurizio De Nisi

Katrin Dobbelaere, Press Office, Théâtre Royal de la Monnaie, Brussels

Jon Finck, Director of Communications, Press Office, San Francisco Opera

Elena Fumagalli, Photo Archive, Teatro alla Scala, Milan

Despina Gadziou

Peter Gelb, General Manager, Metropolitan Opera, New York

Rita Grudzien, formerly of the Press Office, Royal Opera House, Covent Garden

Jacques Herzog and Pierre de Meuron, Herzog & de Meuron

Victoria Huppertz, Press Office, Berlin State Opera

Michiel Jongejan, Press Coordinator, Netherlands Opera, Amsterdam

Selianthe Kallimopoulos, Brand Image, Viktor & Rolf

Isabelle Konikoff, Press Office, Emanuel Ungaro, Paris

Caroline Lebar and Jonathan Zlatics, Lagerfeld Gallery, Paris

Perryn Leech, Houston Grand Opera

Jason Loeffler, Watermill Foundation & Robert Wilson

Sarah Meers, Viktor & Rolf

Luciano Messi, Sferisterio

Marta Monaco, Press Office, Prada, Milan

Neil Parkinson, Special Collections Manager, Library, Royal College of Art

Nicholas Payne, formerly Director of Opera, Royal Opera House, Covent Garden

Pier Luigi Pizzi

Jean Philippe Pons

Press Office, English National Opera, London

Press Office, Metropolitan Opera, New York

Andrew Sinclair

Carla Sozzani, 3 Rooms, Milan

Antonis Stephanou, Press Office, Athens Megaron

Pavlos Tsogounoglou

Julika Weinecker, formerly of the Press Office, Berlin State Opera

Edward Wilensky, Director of Media Relations, San Diego Opera

Robert Wilson

Esther Zumsteg, Herzog & de Meuron.

CREDITS

Quotations from Renée Fleming and John Galliano cited on pp. 6, 8 and 9 were published in American *Vogue*, September 2008. The *Sunday Times* quotation on p. 6 is from the edition published 15 January 1995. The local newspaper quotation on p. 12 is from *The Independent*, 20 January 1995; the quotation from Giorgio Armani cited on p. 13 is from the *International Herald Tribune*, 17 January 1995; the quotation from Jackie Galloway cited on pp. 14–15 was published in the *Sunday Times*, 15 January 1995; the *Musical Times* quotation on p. 15 is from the edition published April 1995. The interview with Marc Bohan quoted on p. 27 was with the fashion journalist Sandy Tsantakis for the Greek television channel Seven X. The Karl Lagerfeld quotation on p. 71 regarding conditions at Balmain was published in American *Bazaar*, January 1993. The interview with Pierre Audi cited on p. 101 was published in the *Los Angeles Times*, 20 July 2008. The quotation from Miuccia Prada cited on p. 103 was published in the *Financial Times*, 28 February 2010. The Gianni Versace quotations on p. 156 were published respectively in *The Times*, 5 January 1995, and the *International Herald Tribune*, 8 January 1991; the quotation on p. 157 regarding childhood memories was published in *The Sunday Times*, 6 January 1991; the quotations on p. 158 were published respectively in *The European*, 4 January 1991, and the *Sunday Times*, 6 January 1991; the quotations on p. 162 were published respectively in the *International Herald Tribune*, 8 January 1991, and *The Times*, 5 January 1991; the Kiri Te Kanawa quotation on pp. 162–63 was published in *The Times*, 5 January 1991.

p. 1 sketch courtesy Helena Matheopoulos; 2–3 © Archivio Fotografico, Teatro alla Scala; 4–5 photo Stephan Olson; 7 photo Ken Howard; 13, 14, 15, 19 sketches courtesy of Giorgio Armani; 16–17, 18, 19, 20, 21 photos by Bill Cooper; 25, 26, 30, 31, 34, 35 sketches courtesy of Marc Bohan; 26, 27, 30, 32, 33, 34, 35 photos Stefanos Kyriacopoulos; 28, 29 photos Claude Mac Burnie; 39, 40, 41, 42, 44, 46, 47, 49, 50, 52, 53, 54, 55, 56, 57, 61, 62, 63 sketches courtesy of Christian Lacroix; 41, 43 photos Ken Howard; 45 photo courtesy of Opéra National de Paris; 48 photo courtesy of Arènes de Nîmes; 51, 55, 57 photos Johan Jacobs Beeldwereld; 58–59, 60, 61, 62–63 photos Monika Rittershaus; 67, 70, 71, 77 sketches courtesy of Opéra de Monte Carlo; 68, 69, 72, 73 sketches Archivio Storico, Maggio Musicale Fiorentino; 74, 75 photos Lelli/Masotti, © Archivio Fotografico, Teatro alla Scala; 76, 77 photos Claude Mac Burnie; 78–79, 80, 81 photos Ken Howard; 80 sketch courtesy of Karl Lagerfeld; 85, 86, 90, 91, 92, 96, 97 sketches courtesy of Rosita and Ottavio Missoni; 87, 88–89, 93, 94–95, 97 photos © Archivio Fotografico, Teatro alla Scala; 101, 103, 104, 105, 109, 110 sketches courtesy of Miuccia Prada; 106–7, 108, 109, 110, 111 photos Ken Howard; 115, 116, 117, 118, 119, 120, 121, 122, 124–25, 126, 127, 131, 132, 133 sketches courtesy of Zandra Rhodes; 123, 125 photos Ken Howard; 128–29, 130, 132, 133 photos Tristram Kenton; 137, 138, 141, 142, 143, 144, 145, 146, 151 sketches courtesy of Emanuel Ungaro; 140 photo courtesy of Luciano Messi; 141, 147, 148, 149, 150, 151, 152, 153 photos Luciano Romano; 156, 159, 162, 172 below, 173 sketches courtesy of John Cox; 157, 160, 161, 164, 167, 170, 172 above Versace/Royal College of Art, London; 165 sketch courtesy of Watermill Foundation & Robert Wilson; 165 photo Stephan Olson; 166, 167 photos Lelli & Mesotti, Teatro alla Scala; 168–69, 171, 172, 173 photos Bill Cooper; 177, 179 photos Dennis Yenmez; 180, 181, 183, 184, 185, 186–87 photos Lesley Leslie-Spinks; 181, 182 sketches courtesy of Viktor & Rolf; 192 photo Ken Howard.

INDEX

Helena Matheopoulos is a writer and lecturer on the subjects of fashion and opera, and has been special adviser on several operatic productions. International Editor-at-Large for Greek *Vogue* and a regular contributor to *The Times*, *Gramophone* and *Opera Now*, she has published several books, including *Maestro: Encounters with Conductors of Today*, *Bravo: Today's Tenors, Baritones and Basses Discuss Their Roles*, *Diva: Today's Sopranos and Mezzos Discuss Their Art*, *Diva: The New Generation* and *Placido Domingo: My Roles in Opera*. She lives in London.

Cover
Front: Sketch made by Christian Lacroix for Attilia in Francesco Cavalli's *Eliogabalo* at the Théâtre Royal de la Monnaie, Brussels, 2004. Courtesy Christian Lacroix and Théâtre Royal de la Monnaie. Back: Soprano Juliane Banse as Agathe, wearing Viktor & Rolf's 'Bouquet' dress in Robert Wilson's production of Carl Maria von Weber's *Der Freischütz*, Baden-Baden, 2009. Photo Lesley Leslie-Spinks.

p. 1 Sketch made by Christian Lacroix for Helena Matheopoulos of a silk faille dress, overlaid with gold lace and copper lamé, and with velvet belt, designed for Teresa Berganza for the Bastille Day Gala in Paris, 14 July 1989; pp. 2–3 The unnamed woman in Arnold Schoenberg's *Erwartung*, conducted by Claudio Abbado, with costumes by Giorgio Armani, La Scala, Milan, 1980–81; pp. 4–5 Scene from Richard Strauss's *Salome*, produced by Robert Wilson, with costumes by Gianni Versace, La Scala, Milan, 1987; right Renée Fleming in a costume by Christian Lacroix for a gala performance of an act from *La traviata*, Metropolitan Opera, New York, 2009.

First published in the United Kingdom in 2011
by Thames & Hudson Ltd, 181A High Holborn,
London WC1V 7QX

Copyright © 2011 Helena Matheopoulos

British Library Cataloguing-in-Publication Data
A catalogue record for this book is available from the British Library

ISBN 978-0-500-51576-1

Printed and bound in China by C&C Offset Printing Co Ltd

To find out about all our publications, please visit
www.thamesandhudson.com. There you can
subscribe to our e-newsletter, browse or download
our current catalogue, and buy any titles that are in print.